MARIJUANA & GROWING SECRETS 2 IN 1

MARIJUANA & GROWING SECRETS 2 IN 1

CALVIN NEWMAN

CONTENTS

MARIJUANA GROWING SECRETS

PSILOCYBIN MUSHROOMS

Part I
WHY PSILOCYBIN MUSHROOMS?

MARIJUANA GROWING SECRETS

THE ULTIMATE BEGINNER'S GUIDE TO PERSONAL AND MEDICAL MARIJUANA CULTIVATION INDOORS AND OUTDOORS. DISCOVER HOW TO GROW TOP QUALITY WEED AND ADVANCED CANNABIS GROWING TIPS

INTRODUCTION

Just like any other kind of gardening, cannabis growing is a skill that is developed over time. Think of cultivating Marijuana as a rewarding hobby that doubles up as a great business opportunity. It is not only easy to learn but also takes a lifetime to master.

Well, don't get me wrong; I am not saying that you should not get started. There is no reason for you to get intimidated. One thing I love about the cultivation of Marijuana is that the process is straight-forward and inexpensive.

One of the best places to start your Marijuana growing journey is to understand the fundamentals of Marijuana cultivation. When you make informed decisions every step of the way, you will have the upper hand at maximizing yields. This is precisely what this guide will help you achieve – an excellent knowledge based on becoming an expert marijuana gardener.

The very first thing you need to think about is where you would like to set up your growing area/space. Well, just because you are thinking "indoors" does not mean that you must have a typical grow room. If you don't have so much space to spare in your home, you don't have to worry because you can still do your grow outdoors – where you have ease of access while still maintaining discretion from nosey neighbors.

If you choose to do indoor growing of Marijuana and you don't have so much space inside your home, you can do it even in an old cabinet in the garage, tent, cabinet, or an unfinished basement. The most important thing is that space is enough to accommodate all your growing equipment required.

If you are just getting started, it is essential to start small. Starting small makes the setting up less costly. Additionally, you make it easier for yourself to monitor a few plants as a beginner. In case you make a mistake, it is also less expensive. As a beginner, there are several challenges you might encounter during your cultivation – like pests and diseases – which ultimately might result in the loss of your marijuana plants. If you have a small space, you will lose to say five plants, which is less expensive compared to losing 50 plants.

That said, it is essential to think big when allocating space for your cultivation. As yourself whether you have enough room for the lights, fans, ducting, and equipment. Do you have some elbow room to move around once the plants are grown? Bear in mind that once the cannabis plants grow, they triple in size and need space.

You may be wondering, "what are some of the fundamentals of growing marijuana?"

Well, here is what you need to know;

Light: If you are growing your plants outdoors, then this should not be a big problem as you depend on night and day for natural regulation of light required by your plants. If you are going to cultivate healthy marijuana plants indoors, you must consider over 12-hours of light in every 24-hr period. Growing indoors means that you have to control light.

Growing medium: when doing organic growing, you will need some soil each time. However, one thing you must bear in mind is that soil is not the only choice. There are neutral mediums that are entirely nutrient-dependent or purely hydroponic – do not use mediums at all.

Air: for your marijuana plants to be healthy, they require a proper gaseous exchange. Unlike outdoors, where this is not an issue of concern, indoor cannabis plants need to take in the fresh air every time. A lack of proper gas exchange channels will encourage molds, pests' weak growths, or even stunted plant growths.

Water: just like every living thing, cannabis plants require water for growth. For outdoor plants, you can depend on rainfall or irrigation. Indoors, water is an essential medium for carrying nutrients. Note that unmodified water plays a vital role in flushing hydroponic and soilless systems. You must ensure the pH of the water is right. Hence, you must have a good pH meter as part of your comprehensive grow kit.

Temperature: while Marijuana is a very hardy plant that survives cold and heat, the truth is that it too can get stressed and not thrive in extremes. Trust me; it can freeze or boil to death! The good thing with growing them indoors is that you can set the required temperatures using fans, heating, and cooling mats, as well as air conditioning units. Realize that lights generate heat too, and that needs to be vented well.

Nutrients: this is the fuel cannabis plants require to fuel growth. Your growth medium rich with compost, living organisms, minerals, and vitamins supply your cannabis plants with adequate foods for their entire lifecycle. The plant's lifeblood is a pre-formulated nutrient blend customized for cannabis if you choose to work with hydroponic systems.

That said, this guide will help you ensure that all the fundamentals are taken care of throughout the lifecycle of your cannabis plant – from vegetative, flowering, and fruiting stages. By the time you are done reading this book, you will not only know about growing but also harvesting and keeping proper amounts on hand throughout the year.

Trust me; this is your key to unlocking big-time yields.

Read on to find out more!

CHOOSE THE STRAIN

When preparing to plant your marijuana strains, whether indoors or outdoors, you must clear a space for the growth area. Whether it is choosing the kind of grow lights to go for or the coveted strains for your setup, you must understand that prepping each grows is critical for your gardening success.

Throughout this chapter, we will discuss how you can choose your strains before getting started with planting. Realize that different plants are different, which requires that you prepare the right growing environment for each strain.

For instance, cannabis Sativa plants are known to grow tall and give off smaller buds during harvest times. Cookie strains and Kushes, on the other hand, tend to grow bushy and give fatter buds during harvest times. The difference in their growth indicates that each one of them requires a unique growing environment, training methods, and nutrition for them to give the kind of yield you desire.

This is why we recommend that you perform thorough research on the kind of strain you wish to plant so that you can go for the best strain you can give the appropriate growth conditions. Luckily for you, you will not have to go to a library to get this information because this book offers you comprehensive coverage of what you need to know – all-under one roof!

Are you not sure what to look for?

Here are some of the key aspects you must consider when looking for the perfect strain for you to grow;

THE OVERALL SIZE OF THE FULL-GROWN PLANT

Just as we have mentioned above, the size of your strain should be your guide when choosing the grow room/space size and the lighting required.

Room size

Knowing the full-grown size of the marijuana strain you want to plant goes a long way in determining the kind of space you need to use. The size of the plant also gives you an idea of how many plants you can grow in a given size, and hence the expected yield.

Lighting

Once you know the size of the plant you want to grow, the next thing is to figure out the amount of lighting it requires. If your plants get too strong light, they might fry to death. On the other hand, if the light is weak, your plants risk not growing at all. Based on the plant size and how many your grow space can take, you can easily determine the amount of light needed and how to position your plants in your grow area.

Average yields

You must have an idea of the yield your strain of choice gives as far as size, quality, and quantity goes. Take a minute to ask yourself these questions;

Will the harvest consist of smaller or fatter buds? If the expected buds are bigger, then this means that they require more nutrition and lighting. You must know what to get in terms of the harvest to ensure that you offer all your plants the time and nutrition they need.

How much yield should you expect? Based on research, the expected yield is based on how well you care for your plants. However, there is a realistic expectation you must keep in mind during growing. In other words, if you expect huge yields from strains that normally do not give big yields, you are setting yourself up for disappointment. That means that you must choose a strain that will give you your expected yield.

LONG DAY PLANTS VS. SHORT DAY PLANTS

The next thing is to determine whether your strain of choice is a long day or short-day plant. If it is a short-day plant, then they require good amounts of darkness and short durations of exposure to light. On the other hand, long-day plants require long durations of light exposure and short periods of darkness.

You must understand this because every plant type requires unique feeding, environmental conditions, lighting, and hence do not mix well with others.

FLOWERING TIMES

This is one of the most important factors to consider when choosing a strain – especially for a beginner cannabis grower like you. Realize that certain plants take longer to flower compared to others. However, if you are not sure how long your plant's flowering period takes, the chances are that you will cut them too early or let them flower for too long and eventually underwhelm the harvest.

Checking the genetics of the plants is not just about the species of the plant you choose. Instead, it is about what state you receive the genetics. These two factors will help you start your plant life on the right track;

Seeds

Starting your garden the old-fashioned seeds-in-the-ground way, allows you to open the future to lots of benefits. For instance, seeds are known to be perfect for beginner growers. This is because they bring you closer to your plants to make a better grower once you know how things are done naturally.

The other thing you need to note is that seeds are the source of all genetics. It does not matter whether you create your strains or desire to hone in on new traits of a certain trait. The most important thing is that you must breed your plants. While seeds are not necessarily 100% pure during the start of your planting, they are very important when breeding and enhancing strains.

Additionally, when you start planting right from the seeds, you pave the way for more resilient plants. Bear in mind that the job of a clone is to grow an entire plant from one clipping. When you are working with clones, you are starting from a restoration stage – something that can be taxing if you go for the wrong clip. Simply start from seeds and ensure that you keep them well-maintained. This way, you end up with stronger plants.

Clones

When you work with clones, you get up and running as fast as possible. This is the reason most growers opt for clones instead of seeds. While seeds offer you stronger plants, the truth is that they cannot tell you the plant's sex until it is too late.

When working with clones, there is no need to pop seeds and waste them. If you pop the wrong seeds and then they don't grow or end up getting plants you did not want in the first place, clones will already be on their way to becoming full-grown plants. They are identical to the plants they were clones from, so you already know the plant's sex and whether or not it is what you want. This is how you make the best clones for your grow.

Therefore, if you are looking for a quick turn-around, clones are the way to go. The truth is, popping seeds and letting them grow can be very tricky, and even if clones are tricky too, rooting them can be done pretty fast.

How to differentiate female Marijuana from male plants

Male Cannabis

Male plants generate mainly pollen needed for the natural reproduction of cannabis plants; seeds appear when male plants are present in the mixture. You'll need a male plant if you want to produce your seeds. However, if you grow ordinary plants and want to pick flowers, we recommend getting rid of any males as soon as possible. You can't distinguish them from each other until they start to flower when the plants start revealing their sex.

"Balls" grow on male weeds, which are open to pollen release and eventually become like a small bouquet. Before this happens, you need to get rid of that road. If they succeed in releasing pollen, it will be too late. An explosion will take three weeks to complete. If you still don't know how to distinguish between them, male flowers don't have pestels at all.

Female Cannabis

Female plants are what everyone needs when growing cannabis, as they produce the kidneys that are part of the plant that contains the highest amount of THC. With just one male plant and a little pollen, your plants can end up filling their flowers with seeds. If you grow male and female plants in the same growing zone, the buds grown there will only produce seeds, so you cannot smoke them.

You can distinguish females because their flowers are not completely closed, they are quite open, and they have small hairs called pestles. They are incredibly easy to recognize because the first thing they produce is their pistils, which male plants do not have at all.

Hermaphrodite Cannabis

Hermaphrodites are a type of plant that includes both male and female flowers, so they will grow buds, but these buds and other plants will also be pollinated. Because of stress, plants may spontaneously become hermaphrodites or convert to them. This can roll over both female and male plants. Thai strains are more genetically prone to becoming hermaphrodites, though, with enough stress, any strain can rollover.

Many factors can cause stress in your plants and ultimately turn them around, such as extra light when they should be in the night cycle, too much or too little water, certain insects or pathogens, watering with cold water, or even a poorly done transplant. Hermaphrodites are not the best type of plants to store, as they can produce buds, but this is a risk because they can fertilize the rest of the plants.

It may seem confusing, but telling male and female weed plants apart is not hard; they are quite different. Planting regular seeds has its advantages. Feminization has its inconveniences; with feminized plants, you can get much bigger yields as you are guaranteed no male plants.

Although, remember that feminized seeds haven't been through a 100 percent natural process of becoming female, which can affect your weed's quality. This is why many cannabis connoisseurs have not yet made the leap from normal to feminized; they tend to reap slightly less yield, which is more potent and delicious.

BEST STRAINS FOR INDOOR GROWING

Now that you know how to choose the strain for you to grow, the next step is to choose the best strains in the market. One of the common questions I hear people asking all time is, "are all strains suitable for indoor grow?"

Well, the answer is YES!

The slightly longer version of this response is, yes, you can grow any strain you wish as long as you know that you can maintain them within the right conditions – climate, nutrition, space, and lighting, among others.

That said, the viability of all strains outdoors is quite a different story because of plant sensitivity. Most of the plants you would wish to plant outdoors may not stand the chill if you live in a colder climate for most of the year.

Beyond the climatic condition, there is also the issue of pests and diseases. In other words, if certain bugs find your plants outside so defenseless, then they are as good as gone! And even when you try to get rid of pests, your plants' quality will significantly decline.

So, what are the best strains for both indoor and outdoor grow – with conditions maintained constant as needed?

Strain #1 Critical

This is a perfect all-rounder, and I would recommend it mostly for outdoor growers aiming for extremely higher yields within a short flowering period. The good news is that the indoor growers can also plant them with a huge yield of approximately $600g/m^2$. They have strong narcotic stone because of about 18% THC levels and are said to be highly genetically stable – consisting of Skunk and Afghani genetics.

So, what makes it a great choice for indoor growers?

This is because it yields a higher harvest within a short flowering period of between 7 and 8 weeks. They are also vigorous and resilient with high-quality yields.

Royal Gorilla

This was once only available to smokers in the US. However, it has since crossed the pond allowing growers to enjoy all the amazing traits this strain has to offer. It is a clean split between two strains – Indica and Sativa. It has a THC content of between 24-27% offering users an impressive wave of cerebral relaxation.

Its taste finds roots in the forest and showcases its earthiness, pungent hits, and pine as it grows beautifully in the great outdoors. It takes about 9-10 weeks to flower. Once the flowering takes place, they give off hefty buds with bright green leaves. Because of their high resin content, they shine bright in the light and reach 90-160 com with an expected yield of between 500-550g/m^2.

With this strain, you are sure of a high-quality product.

Green Gelato

While most growers prefer starting with seeds, if you are looking for something to grow, you can go for the Green Gelato cultivars. It is a blend of Mint girl scout cookies and sunset sherbet. This combination is what makes this strain of cannabis salivating with a whopping THC content of 27%. It tastes like desserts with a perfect blend of citrusy and sweet notes with an earthy tone.

When growing this lady, you must regularly prune the plant using such techniques as fimming, topping into play, ScrOG, LST, or main-lining. Using this causes a clear high that is more physical, considering that there is slightly more Indica than Sativa in it.

Amnesia haze

This is one of the best strains with a flowering period of 10-11 weeks. The fact that you wait for a couple more weeks compared to other strains is accompanied by tremendous benefits as far as effects, potency, and flavor of the product is concerned. It has a THC content of 22% that is accompanied by haze freshness and a fruity flavor.

It has a powerful effect that feels like a parabolic flight into the stratosphere. This effect is accompanied by a rush of euphoria and a strong uplifting head high that makes you feel no effect of gravity whatsoever!

MEDICAL BENEFITS OF MARIJUANA

Humans who have cannabinoid receptors housed within their body which are prepared to bind with cannabinoids located in the Marijuana grow benefit from healing advantages for a range of illnesses. In reality, cannabinoid receptors are contained in humans before birth, and the ingredients are present in a mother's breast milk. Medical marijuana gains merit if you think about your body to be naturally tuned to interact with cannabinoids, and much more so if you acknowledge the increasing evidence of advantages to marijuana usage.

Digestion and Marijuana are no secret. Encountering "the munchies" is among the most apparent marijuana clichés. Regardless of the foolish connotation, studies suggest the endocannabinoid system helps modulate appetite. This is particularly good for the therapy of eating disorders. In reality, research published in the International Journal of Eating Disorders implied that cannabinoids might prove good at dealing with anorexia.

Pain Management

Chronic pain is among the most typical problems that make physicians prescribe medical Marijuana. A recently available survey published in the Spine Journal discovered that one out of five individuals in a Colorado spine facility had been using Marijuana to handle their pain. Of those who used it, nearly 90% said it moderately or greatly relieved their pain.

Mental Health

A typical misconception of Marijuana is the fact that it has detrimental effects on mental health. It's feasible that excessive doses of tetrahydrocannabinol (THC) could cause anxiety in certain individuals, as well as many who think it can expedite the beginning of predisposed personality problems. Still, these facts are yet to be established virtually by any respected studies.

The latest trend in the psychological health field has been investigating the human relationship with Marijuana. In turn, research has linked cannabinoids to a selection of psychological health concerns. The study catalog continues to be growing.

Not merely has Marijuana been associated with the brain wellbeing, cannabinoid receptor activity in mind before birth implies the compounds might be involved in mind growth. Marijuana was connected to the development of new neurons in the human brain, or maybe neurogenesis, and total brain plasticity.

Cancer treatment

It has long been recommended to fight the unwanted side effects of chemotherapy. Still, Oncologists throughout the planet are focusing on trials to find out if Marijuana may be utilized for treating cancer itself. Numerous individuals decide to grab the Rick Simpson Oil treatment program to remedy cancer, but there are lots of diverse techniques of going about the therapy.

What to Consider Before Trying Medical Marijuana

Constantly inform your doctor about any vitamins, dietary supplements, herbs, and over-the-counter medications you are using, including medical Marijuana. In case you reside in a state in which medical marijuana is legal, and would prefer talking to somebody who's effectively utilizing medical Marijuana for treating unwanted side effects of breast cancer, you must question your care team about linking you with an additional individual.

Insurance, Medicare, and Medicaid don't cover medical Marijuana. The price of medical Marijuana can start at approximately a hundred dollars per month and may be higher, depending on just how much is required. The main point here is the fact that medical Marijuana could be costly.

THC and CBD exist in levels that are different in various strains of Marijuana. THC, as well as CBD each, offer various benefits. For instance, CBD might be better at easing discomfort, while THC might be better at controlling nausea.

You'll probably need to perform a great deal of investigation by yourself to discover the ratio of CBD to THC that works ideal for managing your side effects. This could rather take a good deal of trial and error. What works for somebody else might not work for you.

You might need to visit many medical marijuana dispensaries until you come across one you are at ease with and possesses staff members who could respond to all your questions about the amounts of THC and CBD in the strains offered. Based on the laws in your state, some dispensaries might cater far more to recreational users than medical users. Health dispensaries are usually much more medical and also have staff members that are much more apt to get experience assisting individuals with cancer medical marijuana use for treating unwanted side effects.

It can be beneficial to contact the dispensary and explain the unwanted side effects you have, along with any experience you have had with Marijuana, and get if you could plan a consultation appointment and have a staff member. When you are at all uncomfortable, go to an alternative dispensary.

Several physicians who often recommend medical Marijuana recommend asking the dispensary team member several basic questions before you begin chatting specifically about your side effects:

- Is your Marijuana farmed using pesticides?
- Are your items stored and also handled correctly to stay away from contamination and spoilage?
- Are your products tested for bacteria and fungus? What exactly are the effects?
- Are your products tested for amounts of pesticides?
- What's your experience and training for recommending medical Marijuana?
- Perhaps, have you worked with cancer patients before?

Several oncologists have suggested that their patients attend a medical marijuana dispensary, instead of an outlet that caters to leisurely users. There's no study on if recreational Marijuana is as useful and safe for cancer patients as they are generally costlier healthcare grade range. However, several dispensaries take additional care to make sure there aren't any mold or pesticides in their medical-grade Marijuana.

If you work for the federal government, a federal government contractor, or maybe an employer that conducts frequent drug tests, you might face disciplinary action for utilizing medical Marijuana. Check your employer's medical marijuana policy before you begin making use of it.

In case you are a part of a clinical trial, there is a lot of unknown about how the ingredients in medical Marijuana might communicate with any experimental drugs. It will make great sense to speak with the physician coordinating the trial before you attempt any medical marijuana.

2

CHOOSE YOUR GROW ROOM/SPACE/GREENHOUSE

Once you figure out what strain you would like to plant and how you wish to start the garden, the next important thing is to determine where you would like to grow them in the first place.

Ask yourself whether you intend to buy a grow tent, build a greenhouse, or you are going to plant them on the ground outside. Do you intend to convert one of the rooms in the house into a grow room?

These questions are very important in ensuring that you have thoroughly thought of everything when getting the pots, clones, or seeds before getting started. However, before you delve into finding out the sort of housing you would like to plant your marijuana plants, it is important to reflect on the area of plants you intend to light – otherwise referred to as canopy of your growth.

To do this, you must follow these approaches;

HOW MUCH SPACE DO YOU WANT TO ALLOCATE FOR YOUR GROW ROOM?

If you want to know how big your garden is going to be, you must know the grow space limitations. Before going ahead to buy the bags of seeds or clones, take time to measure the grow area you wish to use in growing your marijuana plants. This way, you will have an idea of how many plants your space can hold.

HOW MANY PLANTS CAN YOU GROW IN THAT SPACE?

One good rule of thumb you must remember is that if you feel you are not sure how they grow buckets are going to be in the growing area, consider giving your plants at least 2-4 square feet in that space. Then divide that number by 2,3, and 4 to find out how many full-grown plants can grow there comfortably.

Ensure that the minimum you can go is at least 1 square foot. Try using a few buckets to measure it yourself.

Once you have measured out your grow space, and have an idea of what it will take to grow your garden, the next thing you should think about is how you plan to house them. There are three types of houses you can use for your plants;

Grow tents

This is one of the most common houses among indoor marijuana growers. They are not only increasingly convenient but also a manageable way of housing your plants. It does not matter whether you set it up in the garage or anywhere else in the house if you need a tent the size of a room, you can get it to accommodate all the plants you want to grow.

The good thing is that tents come in various sizes and styles for any grower and nearly all the plants you wish to plant. With a tent, there is no need to drill hanging hooks or vents for fans and lightings. What I like most about them is that you have superior control over the growing environment as opposed to many other setups.

Grow room

It does not matter whether you are going to set it up in the bedroom, closet, garage, or any other room in your apartment. The truth is that you can utilize your own space the way you see fit. Think of it as a much more convenient way of growing your plants than having to buy a tent.

With a grow room, you can get fresh air in fast and circulate it naturally throughout your garden.

One thing you must bear in mind is that grow rooms do not need one to purchase a whole tent. All you need to buy are reflective materials and fans to convert your room – something that is way cheaper than buying a tent. This also depends on the canopy you intend to grow.

Using grow rooms allow you to utilize the space that is already available to you. This includes windows with proper ventilation and power outlets. Trust me; there is not much to buy when converting a room into a grow room fit for your plants. The other thing is that once you have the right setting, you can use extra light from the sun to supplement the lights, especially when power is out.

Greenhouse

When doing indoor growing of your marijuana plants, you can consider using greenhouses when you don't have tons of room inside or outside either. You can think of either building or buying a greenhouse. The good thing with using a greenhouse is that you enjoy the same benefits as the outdoors – abundance of light and temperatures – with the added benefit of supplemental lighting and ventilation. When you grow crops in greenhouses, you not only save money on lighting by accessing the light from the sun, which is the optimal light source.

If you need more lighting, you can go for T5's or HID with lower power to back you up until the sun comes out whenever you have blackouts. You can also use plant training techniques such as light dep to get bigger plants from greenhouses. Because they are already accli-mated to outdoor surroundings, you can take greenhouse plants out and plant outside. You don't need much training here.

3

CHOOSE YOUR MEDIUM

Once you know what strain you plan to grow and where you want it grown, then the next thing you must think about is the growth medium to use – which is the most important stage of preparation. The medium you choose to use will determine how many nutrients you need to include, the type of nutrients suited for your plants, how to feed your plants, and how to overcome challenging situations whenever they arise.

There are at least three popular grow mediums to choose from. Each grow medium has its advantages and disadvantages. That is why you must exercise caution to ensure that you make the right decision before growing your plants.

SOIL

This is one of the most used all-purpose mediums that is perfect for the growing of marijuana plants. The good thing with using soil as a growing medium is that it does not need much supplemental nutrition considering that they are already loaded with high-quality nutrients.

If you consider mixing your super soil, you end up eliminating about 90% of supplemental nutrients. Soil is already loaded with the nutrients you need for your plant's life.

Soil is great for beginners because it has a lot of buffer room about readings and feedings. It retails nutrients that are best for all mediums. Your plants need little nutrients when they are just starting to grow, and when they need more, you just need to add a little.

That said, growing your plants in the soil means that they are generally going to take longer to grow. Additionally, if the soil has nutrient issues, they might not show up immediately, and when they do, it can be hard to fix them. The truth is, your plants risk getting so sick in the soil beyond repair when there is an issue there, and you don't know what it is.

Unlike the hydroponic systems where the whole plant roots hang down in a bucket, roots in the soil go all over the place, and when you don't have enough room for them, you end up with root-bound plants – and those are not good at all!

Getting the Soil Right

Anyone who has tried any type of gardening will understand the importance of getting the soil conditions right. The soil is where your plant will gather the necessary nutrients to grow. There are also different types of soil; texture and drainage can make a huge difference.

Good soil for your marijuana plant will have a light texture and be fairly good at retaining water. If the soil is heavy, the plant roots will struggle to spread, and there will be too much water for the healthy development of the plant.

Generally, it is not advisable to simply go outside and dig some of your soil; it will probably not be beneficial for your marijuana plant. Instead, you should look at purchasing a potting soil. This is soil that has been specially formulated to provide young plants with all the nutrients they need to get them started using this **feeding schedule.**

Some of the ingredients you could have in your soil include;

Perlite - This is a common addition to soil and one that you could easily add to a standard bag of soil purchased in your local garden center. It looks like little white rocks, and it will increase water's ability to drain through your soil, preventing you from overwatering your plant. Also, it encourages oxygen into the soil for your plants. However, you shouldn't use too much of this if you are planning to add nutrients to your soil; keep it to 10% of your soil mix.

Bone Meal - A bone meal is high in phosphorous and calcium, which are great for your plants as they start to flower. However, it a slow-releasing fertilizer, so it's best to be mixed in your soil when you start potting. The nutrients will then be available when they are ready to flower.

Composted Humus - This is any type of compost that has naturally decomposed. Because natural materials have been broken down, it is full of nutrients that will benefit your plants.

It also benefits your plant by helping the soil to retain moisture and oxygen. The result is better quality soil for your plants.

Bat Guano - This is a great way to add nutrients to your soil. Simply sprinkle it on the top of the soil and keep it moist. This will encourage bacteria to feed on the guano and break it down to create the nutrients your plants need. It can be used throughout the entire growing cycle.

Vermiculite - This is a good addition if you are losing water too quickly in your plants. A little will help to slow down the drainage and can make the soil heavier. But it will also restrict the addition of oxygen to the soil.

Worm Castings - These are full of nutrition that is essential and extremely beneficial to your marijuana plants. There are no real downsides to adding this to your soil. It can make a valuable addition regularly to encourage good microbes and provide nutrients for your growing plants.

Pumice - Pumice is a type of volcanic rock. Because it is porous, it is good at holding water and allowing airflow. It works similarly to perlite and should be mixed with your soil.

Kelp - Kelp is a plant in itself and, as such, contains all the nutrients that every plant needs to survive. This makes it a great addition to your soil for encouraging plant growth.

It is also extremely beneficial as it is excellent at repelling slugs and other pests from your Marijuana while keeping the soil moist. You can cover your soil throughout the growth of your plant, but only after it has germinated, you don't want to suffocate it as well as the weeds!

Once you have got your soil sorted, you now need to consider fertilizers. If you plan on repotting your plants regularly, this might not be necessary as the fresh soil will have its nutrients. But, if this is not the case, fertilizers are essential to ensure your plants have everything they need to grow big and strong!

It is possible to mix your fertilizers. However, unless you are certain about what is already in your soil, this can be a dangerous process. Homemade fertilizers can react with chemicals in the soil and cause a detrimental effect on your plant.

As a beginner, you should purchase one of the many fertilizers on the market. This will help you to choose the right one for the stage of plant growth. A general fertilizer works well for seedlings, but flowering plants must have balanced nutrition.

Once you know your soil types and understand your plants' needs, you can use the following as your fertilizer:

Chicken Manure - A little chicken manure can go a long way when looking after your plants; it's full of nutrients essential for all stages of plant growth.

Vinegar - Did you know that one drop of white vinegar on baking soda will release carbon dioxide, which your plants thrive on.

A good way of doing this is to put the vinegar in a plastic bag and hang it over the bowl. Prick a tiny hole to allow it to drip out slowly. But, you must do this in a way that keeps the carbon dioxide in the space; this is not good for outside growing. There will also be a heavy smell of vinegar that you won't want others noticing.

Kitchen Waste - All the organic food waste you usually chuck away can be put into a pile to encourage them to decompose. Once they start to decompose, you can put them on the top layer of your soil, releasing all the nutrients your plant needs when you are watering them.

HYDROPONICS

This is an all-water growing medium. It is soil-less, less messy, and whenever you run into nutrient issues, you can fix them faster and easily as opposed to when your plans are grown in soil mediums. The good thing about this growing medium is that it takes less time than soil plants to be harvested.

Growing Marijuana in hydroponics ensures that your plants absorb nutrients faster and grow faster than grown in soil or coco. However, this requires someone who is already advanced to a professional grower.

That said, there is no buffer when growing your marijuana plants in hydroponics. With hydroponic systems, just a single misstep and your plants will feel it. While nutrient issues are much easier to fix, the problem is that you are likely to get more nutrient spikes than you would in soil.

Considering that your plants are essentially in the water at the root level, the basins and water must be checked regularly to prevent the growth of fungus, mold, or root rot that are damaging to the whole plant.

COCO

Think of coco as the perfect middle ground between soil and hydroponics. Even though there is no nutritional value to using coco in growing your plants, however, just like soil, the nutrients added tend to be held longer than when you use hydroponics. This simply means that there is no need to run heavy water flow like you would in a hydro system.

The good thing with coco as a growing medium is that your plants are assured of getting nutrients from the beginning rather than choosing to trust that soil is good enough to carry your plants through to the flowering phase.

Cocos retain nutrients better than hydro systems. However, they don't hold the nutrients longer than soil mediums. The plants take longer to grow compared to the hydro system, but they tend to grow faster than when you are using soil mediums. Using coco coir as your grow medium requires your skill level to be advanced or professional.

What you must note is that the nutrient issues here can be tricky to address because of the semi- retainability of the medium. Here, you also don't have a ton of buffer. Finally, if you fail to break down and mix your coco well, the pH might spike, causing harm to your plants.

4

CHOOSE YOUR GROW LIGHTS

At this point, we are almost through with the vitals of what you require to get started growing your plants. You can take a deep breath because we are almost ready to grow our marijuana plants!

Now, once you are through with this stage, the next thing would be to grab your tools and get down to work – literally. However, before we get down to the easy stuff, we might want to figure out one last thing – the lighting system for growing your plants. This is one of the last things that will determine your yield, the complexity of growing, and the amount of energy your plants will need during growth.

Like most things in your grow room, all kinds of lights you intend to use, have their advantages and disadvantages. Some add a ton of heat to the growing space, while others don't even give enough power.

Others even have too much power without necessarily adding to a degree of temperature to the grow surroundings.

Before you decide to use it to grow your plants, you must take time to understand the benefits and challenges of every lighting option in the market. Here are some of the options and their pros and cons;

HIGH-INTENSITY DISCHARGE (HID) GROW LIGHTS

I love most about the HID because they offer the closest light spectrum to that of the sun. This way, your marijuana plants get the kind of lighting they need for their growth. With this kind of lighting, you are assured of healthy plants right from the beginning to the time when you harvest a huge yield – especially when you take the time to train properly.

They also come in a wide range of reflectors and wattages that suit your growing needs. In short, there is an HID for any application you wish to use it for.

If you just need the lights for standard to grow, then a regular HPS/MH will work perfectly for you. However, if your plants are spaced differently, here is what you can work with;

- 400 watts Grow lights are perfect for 1-3 plants within a 3x3 ft or 2x4 ft of each other.
- 600 watts Grow lights are perfect for 3-4 plants in a 4x4 or 5x5 feet each other.
- 1000 watts are strongest of all the grow lights in this

category and can grow between 5 and 6 plants within 6x6 feet grow area.

That said, it is important to note that double-ended grow lights are much more intense than standard, single-ended bulbs. This is mainly because of the dual base connection they offer, hence firing from two connections instead of one at the base of the bulb.

CMH grow lights, on the other hand, offer an even spectrum of lights without excess red or blue light spectrums. They have ceramic bases that make them more superior to DE lights with similar wattages. Additionally, they can fire at high wattages.

LED GROW LIGHTS

You must bear in mind that giving your plants the exact spectrum of light they need for their growth. LEDs are one of the most incredible ways to give your plants the light they require without necessarily exposing them to excess heat or light spectrums they do not need.

They can pinpoint the precise wavelengths of light your marijuana plants absorb and offer them exactly that. In other words, there is nothing your marijuana plants will waste with LED lights compared to HIDs.

While the yield you get from plants when using LED lights is not as much as you harvest from HIDs, the truth is that LEDs go a long way toward helping your plants give a superior flavor. The product you get is stickier and of high quality too.

Trust me, with LEDs; your marijuana plants will give you properties other grow lights may not give – like IR and UV for resins. The light generated has an intense wavelength. This means that if you move them too close to the plants, you risk bleaching your marijuana plants.

For marijuana plants, Advance Spectrum Max engineer the perfect spectrum for them. Using supplemental grow lights offers you limited spectrum range – either all blue, all red, dual, or a triband. However, if you choose to use LEDs, they will fill the gaps your main lights do not have. Full-spectrum LED grow lights; on the other hand, offer your marijuana plants a wide light spectrum covering all the spectrums your plants will need. The only challenge with HIDs is that they give plants too many spectrums to process – eventually, the plants end up wasting.

LEDs tend to outperform the HIDs in terms of quality – even if they have the same wattage. For instance, if you have a 600 watts LED, it will outperform a 600 Watts HID with a similar spectrum output because of the wide spectrum LEDs give.

T5 GROW LIGHTS

With these kinds of lights, you get a limited amount of heat. They are much similar to the HIDs because they both have "grow" and "bloom" spectrums and so much more. Even though they have limited power and lower-yielding harvests, they are perfect alternatives for marijuana growers who wish to grow their plants without using up too much energy or bleaching the plants as LEDs do.

The good thing with these grow lights is that you can use them to grow close to anything. However, considering that they are not that strong, your plants will remain small. According to research, they run 75% cooler compared to HIDs. The yields, in this case, are small but will get you a pinch of yield at the end of the growing period.

They come in a wide range of sizes hence covering the canopy you wish to grow pretty well. It good when you are growing marijuana, clones, spices, and herbs.

5

TOOLS

Throughout your growing experience, you are going to use lots of tools from scissors, meters, controllers, to gloves, among others. Trust me; there are lots of tools that will make your time in the grow space. While all these tools play important roles in growing your Marijuana and giving you the yields, you have always wanted, some of them are more important than others.

Here are key tools you will need even before you start setting up your grow space;

HYGROMETER

A wide range knows this tool of names, but it is critical for growing your marijuana plants. They help you read the temperatures of your growing space and the level of CO_2 and humidity in your space.

When growing Marijuana indoors, one of the most important things is to be keen on the growing environment.

You will feel how humid or hot the surroundings are, but a hygrometer will tell you precisely what is happening in your marijuana garden. When the conditions are out of range, you can easily and promptly adjust as necessary so that your plants have optimal growth conditions.

PRUNING SHEARS

This is another important tool that will help you take off drying leaves, train your plants, and clipping new clones. Trust me; you will be surprised how important and handy shears can be. They will help you clean cut off your plants, a very important process for the whole plant.

When the plant leaves are not removed as required, it can cause unnecessary damage to the whole plant. Unnecessary damage translates to the plant sending out signals to the rest of the plant sections for healing, hence hindering growth. That also has an impact on the final yield you get.

PH/PPM METERS

It does not matter what growing medium you are using for your growth. What matters most is that you know the pH level of the nutrient-rich water you are using to feed your plants. This ensures that you are not poisoning your plants at all. PPM – also referred to in full as parts per million – are very important, and you must keep an eye on them to ensure that your marijuana plants are not eating too much or too little.

MICROSCOPE

You may be thinking, "isn't this for a research lab?" Well, think of your garden as a lab in itself. When you are growing your marijuana plants, you are researching some sort at different plant growth stages. At one point, you want to know the sex of the plants, the trichomes, and searching for bugs – and what better tool to use than a microscope.

Microscopes will help you spot tiny details or features of your plants every step of the way to ensure that you are on the right track with your growth.

HEAT THERMOMETER

It is always a brilliant idea to know how much heat is in your canopy. However, you cannot know the exact temperature readings if you don't have a thermometer. This is precisely why you must consider investing in a good heat thermometer that can help you read the temperatures of a specific surface or surfaces that are not easy to measure.

6

DAILY MAINTENANCE

It does not matter whether you are growing your plants indoors or outdoors because each day in the garden presents its unique challenges. There are times when the pH and PPM levels spike or the temperatures go out of range – and let us not get started in the pests!

Making the initial investment in growing cannabis is always helpful for growers who have already faced the same issues you might be facing during your first growing experience. Before we proceed, it is important to take note of some of the common mistakes you should avoid;

Overfeeding: It is best to follow the directions provided by the manufacturer.

Overwatering medium-based plants: If you have decided to use buckets/pots for your plants, you will need to use a hefting approach. That is when you judge its weight by 'hefting.' First, you want to judge its dry weight—via hefting. Water, the plant until the water, is running through the drain holes—heft again. When the pot feels the same wet as it did dry, it is time to water again. It is basic common sense.

Over-Analyzing: Watching the 'weed' grow is similar to watching a first-born child. You don't want to miss a single thing. However, don't try to fix every yellow leaf you see; watch out for the big ones.

Overspending on Materials: If you are a beginner, try to stay on a set budget. It is easy to get 'caught up' in the excitement of it all.

CHECK PH LEVELS

If you are working with a hydroponic system, the most important thing is to calibrate your pH meter and the meter used in measuring the water levels in the reservoir. If you are using coco and soil as your grow mediums, ensure that you water your plants. Regularly check the runoff pH levels to ensure that they are optimal as low levels are toxic to the plant and too high lowers the growth of your plants.

This is why you must have a perfect acidity level in the water you have in the reservoirs – something between 5.5 and 6.0. If you don't check the pH and it is too high, your plants will not grow as you want them to. Simply use pH downs to bring it back to optimal levels. If the pH is too low, on the other hand, try to regulate it to optimal levels.

Here's how your plants are affected by the pH levels;

- Less or equal to 3.5 – causes plant root damage

- 4.0-4.5 – causes poor nutrient uptake by the plant roots
- 5.0-5.4 – optimal pH level for optimal growth of your marijuana plants
- 5.4-5.8 – also perfect pH levels for your plant growth
- 6.0-7.0 – is acceptable pH levels but you must be keen to ensure that they don't go higher than this leads to poor nutrient uptake by the plant
- 8.5 and above – cause root damage to the plant and decreased growth.

CHECK PPM LEVELS

This is an important element that gives you an idea of how many elements are available for the plants' feeding solution. It is an important factor to keep an eye on ensuring that you are not overfeeding your plants with too many nutrients.

When your plants are young, you don't need to give them too many nutrients because they do not need it. In that case, they could use between 100-250 ppm.

During the first half of the vegging cycle of the plants, ensure that the ppm levels are between 300 and 400. This stage comes right after you transplant the seedlings, and at this point, your plants still do not need too many nutrients.

During the second half of vegging, you must keep the nutrient levels at 450 to 700 ppm. Here, your plants have started needing more nutrients than the first two stages.

During the first half of the flowering stage, ensure that the nutrients are between 750 and 950 ppm. At this stage, your marijuana plants are eating more food because they are actively growing.

During the second half of flowering, they will need even more foods than before and hence the reason to keep the nutrient levels between 1000 and 1600 ppm.

As the flowering stage ends and you get into the harvest season, ensure that the levels are close to 0 as possible. You must flush your plants so that there are no more particles left over.

CHECK GROWS FOR PESTS.

One thing you must remember at all times is that your garden is a pest's grocery store. This means that you must check your plants at least once to ensure that pests are not feasting on your growth. Ensure that you check both the tops and bottoms of the leaves, walls, floors, as well as buckets and grow mediums for pests, fungus, and mold build-up.

This is especially important for your marijuana plants outside and in greenhouses, considering that they are exposed to more pests, fungi, and molds than those growing indoors. Most of the outdoor plants are at risk of rats and rabbits, fungal spores, and high amounts of mold, among other pests.

INSPECT LEAVES FOR SIGNS OF NUTRIENT DEFICIENCIES

When your grow is not getting the right amount of nutrients they require for growth and nourishment, the truth is that they will not get you the yield you need at the end of the harvest season. If your grow space is free of pests, but your plant's leaves are turning yellow/brown, curling, and becoming brittle, the chances are that they are experiencing a deficiency in their nutrition.

Ensure that you check the color of your plant leaves at least once a day. This way, you can easily catch a problem if there is one. Pay close attention to their deficiency charts and nutrient bottles to find out if there are issues. If you find nutrient issues, be sure to supplement your marijuana plants with the missing nutrient or elements needed.

CHECK ENVIRONMENTAL CONDITIONS

Some of the essential environmental conditions for your grow include humidity, temperatures, and CO2 levels. These are the most important factors to keep a close eye on every day because they affect transpiration and photosynthesis processes.

When the lights are off, the acceptable temperature drop should be within 10-15° F. If it is above this, then you know that there is a problem and must be addressed immediately. Here are the correct conditions for every stage of your grow;

- Seedlings and clones – 72-82 $^\circ$ F at a humidity of between 70 and 75%
- Vegging stage – 68-78 $^\circ$ F at a humidity of between 50 and 70%
- Flowering stage – 68-77 $^\circ$ F at a humidity of between 40 and 50%
- Harvest stage – 65-75 $^\circ$ F at a humidity of between 45 and 55%

At this stage, things should be starting to come together. You've chosen the type of Marijuana you wish to grow, pot size, and the type of system you wish to use to grow your Marijuana. For clarity, if you are a beginner, then it is best to start with a pot, good quality soil and some fertilizer. Providing you've chosen the right light set up and understand the light cycles, you're nearly ready to start planting.

First, you need to understand the importance of getting the humidity right, ventilate your crop, and perhaps the most concerning of all, how to prevent Marijuana's aroma penetrating the air. Even if you have just six plants, this aroma might be enough to attract others that would like your crop for their reasons!

You are probably already aware that humidity simply refers to the amount of moisture present in the air. The more there is, the more humid the air.

The marijuana plant is not keen on high levels of moisture; this is good as modern heating systems tend to dry the air in your home. However, nature is all about balance. Low humidity levels equate to high evaporation pressure. This is good as it helps your plants to absorb vital nutrients. However, if the humidity becomes too low, then the plant will assume there is a problem with water and protect itself from dehydration.

Unfortunately, this means it will no longer absorb water and will not be able to grow!

The temperature of your grow room partly controls humidity. It is, therefore, essential to have a humidity meter and consistently monitor it; this will ensure you can react appropriately if the humidity levels change.

You need to know the current humidity rating. It's best to use a hygrometer for this (analog or digital). It is worth noting that the humidity is affected by the temperature outside the house. For instance, temperatures outside below 15° Fahrenheit your humidity reading will probably be about 35%. It should increase by 5% every time the temperature rises by 10°F.

Air-conditioning or a dehumidifier. These are a great way of removing moisture from a room, allowing you to bring it down to the most appropriate level for your needs. Cat litter can be your best friend if the humidity gets too high. Simply spread some in a tray and leave it in the growing room. It attracts moisture and will lower the moisture level in the room.

Add moisture by having water in the room in open bowls; it will evaporate into the room, increasing the humidity levels. Another option is to use a humidifier that will push moisture into your room, helping to boost the moisture level.

You can also use a vaporizer; this uses warm water and vaporizes it into the air, boosting the moisture content, if needed.

Add ventilation; this can reduce the humidity level if the outside air already has a lower humidity rating. A fan, coupled with an atmospheric controller, can make a huge difference to the ease in which you can control the humidity levels. De-leaf some of the plants with the most leaves on. Excessive leaves can increase the humidity in your growing room; this is particularly true when you have limited airflow.

These are all great methods to boost or decrease your moisture levels. However, the key to this approach is making sure that you monitor the levels regularly and adjust them slowly.

Unsurprisingly getting the humidity wrong will affect the growth rate of your plants. But this is not the only sign that there is an issue with humidity:

White powder - This is a fungal disease that only arrives when the atmosphere is too humid. A good airflow system can help to prevent this.

Bud Rot - If your buds' insides are white or brown with mold, then you have bud rot, and your crop is effectively useless. This is incredibly frustrating, and not something that will be an issue if you monitor the humidity rating properly.

Nutrition - If your plants start to look like they have yellow or burnt tips, they are more effectively consuming more water than they should be; this is usually because of low humidity.

Increase the humidity levels immediately. Remember, the right humidity levels will encourage maximum growth!

Choosing the Right Ventilation System

Ventilation is often a difficult issue. The basic truth is that no matter how many or how few plants you are growing, you are likely to be growing them in confined conditions.

There is a good reason for this; you don't want everyone knowing what you are doing. Even when growing them for medical reasons, many people do not realize this is an option and are likely to report you. This will give you unnecessary hassle and highlight to others that you have Marijuana.

You need ventilation for several reasons:

Toxin removal - Marijuana is no different from most plants in that it pushes toxins out of itself through the leaves. Airflow helps to remove these toxins from the plants. Without this, they can stay there, preventing the plant from pushing more out and even encouraging the growth of mold.

Humidity- We already looked at humidity and understood the importance of getting this right. However, as we mentioned, airflow can help with distributing the same humidity level across the room.

A fan can simply move air around your room, helping to decrease the chance of mold forming on your plants. It can also be used to bring air inside from outside the building; this can lower the temperature to reduce the humidity levels. This approach is especially effective if you add a temperature and humidity control device as the fan can switch automatically.

Creating the Ventilation

The most comprehensive method of creating ventilation is through the use of several items:

- An intake fan, this sucks air in from the outside.
- An extractor fan; pushes the air out of your grow room and into the outside world.
- An interior fan moves air across the plants. This might not be necessary if you only have a few plants.
- Some sort of air filter device.

The intake fan does more than just bring air in; it pushes it in at the same rate the extractor is removing it; this allows the air pressure to remain the same, preventing any disruption to the growing cycle of the plants.

CHECK FILTERS IN YOUR GROW ROOMS.

The other daily maintenance, you must pay attention to the filters around the grow space – especially if you are growing your marijuana plants indoors. This way, you ensure that your plants can grow in a clean space free of dust, clogging their stoma. On the other hand, your filter will ensure that you can hide smells from your grow area.

You must note that if you can smell your grow from 3 feet away from the filter or have dust built up in your grow space, the chances are that your plants need an inspection, repair, and a change of filters for a clean one.

Dealing with the aroma

Of course, if you've ever had any experience with growing Marijuana, you'll know it has a distinctive smell, which is relatively easy for others to detect. While ventilation is essential, this will push the plant's smell into your house, not something you are likely to want to risk!

First, you need a fan to remove the air. You should already have this as part of your airflow and humidity control measures. Moving the air outside will reduce the potency of the aroma from your marijuana plants.

But this is not enough; the aroma could still give you away and attract unwanted attention. There are several ways of dealing with the aroma:

Carbon Filter - This is the perfect addition to your extractor fan. All the air leaving your room should be pulled through the fan. In the process, it will need to pass through the carbon filter you have fitted.

Choose a filter that fits perfectly into your exhaust ventilation system (there are sets). The carbon will attract the aroma and hold it, preventing it from getting into the outside world. You do need to have a fan, and you need a quality carbon filter to do the job properly. Searching on eBay or Amazon for a "carbon filter fan" will do the job.

Negative Ions - A more advanced method is to use a negative ion generator. These charges the particles in the air and effectively gives these particles the ability to neutralize the odor in other particles, eliminating the Marijuana's aroma.

A carbon filter is more effective, but this is a great alternative.

HEPA - This is an alternative type of filter that can be used in your grow room. However, it still requires airflow through it. The fan does not need to ventilate outside the grow room, making it an attractive option in some scenarios.

Choose the ventilation system and aroma protection system that suits your needs and budget. This will ensure you monitor the humidity, and your plants will start growing well. It is worth noting that a HEPA filter cannot filter very small particles. You will need a carbon filter for this.

CHECK THE SURFACE FOR EXCESS MOISTURE.

This is often a sign of temperature issues and humidity as well. It could also indicate that there is a problem in the airflow and CO_2 problems.

You must note that excess moisture in the grow area risk your plants of mold and serves as a good breeding ground for harmful bacteria, which will ultimately destroy your plants. If you check your growing areas – basins, reflectors, buckets, and reservoirs, among others – and find out that there is excess moisture, ensure that you completely dry it.

If you are growing your marijuana plant in soil, it is a brilliant idea to check the moisture levels of the soil to ensure that you are feeding the plants as required. Simply stick your finger about ½" to 1" to check for dryness of moisture. Alternatively, you can use a moisture meter. If using cocoa, you can also check for moisture levels the same way.

However, if your grow is in hydroponics, you don't need to measure the moisture content considering your plant is in the water anyways. The best thing is to ensure that your plants are getting sufficient amounts of water. Ensure that the water is not rolling right off the pebbles and Rockwool, leaving your plants dry. At the same time, you must not overpower your plants with water, as this might result in a nutrient lockout.

CHECK THE HEIGHT OF YOUR LIGHTS ABOVE YOUR PLANTS.

You must ensure that the height of your lights is not too close or too far from the plants. Remember what we discussed earlier – not all lights are the same – HID, LEDs, and T5 fluorescent grow lights. All these require different heights.

For instance, if you are using;

HID grow lights

- 1000 watts lights must be between 16-31" from the plants
- 600 watts lights must be positioned 14-25" from the plants
- 400 watts lights must be positioned 12-19" from the plants

T5 fluorescent grows lights must be positioned 5-12" above the plants.

LED grow lights

- 900 watts and above must be positioned 26-42" from a vegging plant
- 600-850 watts lights must be positioned 24-26" from a vegging plant

- 450-550 watts lights must be placed 20-30" away from a vegging plant
- 240-400 watts lights must be 16-30" away from a vegging plant.

That said, you must measure the canopy temperatures to ensure that you don't end up burning your plants or underwhelming plant leaves. The canopy temperatures must be the same throughout you grow space.

7

PRE-VEGGING STAGE

At this point, you are now ready and have the genetics ready to hit the ground. Before you get right to it – the vegging stage – it is important that you get your seeds or clones ready for your future harvest. This is what we refer to as the pre-vegging stage.

How then can you start your Grow from Seeds and Clones?

Once you have your seeds and clippings ready, the first thing is to get them into a growing medium so that they can get started on a healthy journey. You must bear in mind that this stage is where you make or break your seeds/clones. If you get them started on the wrong footing, the chances are that you will pay for it later. This is why you must start your seeds or clones on the right footing for the seedlings' quality when the time comes for transplanting into larger pots.

What happens if you are starting with seeds?

Growing your marijuana plants from seeds is mostly a natural way of starting a garden. However, it is also the most challenging.

One thing you must note is that when seeds start their lives as plants, their taproots come out of the seeds and pops the shell. This allows the roots to penetrate the medium for nutrition. The good thing is that you don't have to use special seeds to grow like you would clones.

There are at least three ways you can do propagation before they get into the vegging stage;

POPPING SEEDS ON PAPER TOWELS

Here, when you pop seeds on moist paper towels, you know whether you have tap grassroots rather than playing the waiting game for your seedlings to finally show up. All you need is to plant the popped seeds in your growth medium, and you are ready to go!

STARTING IN CELLS

Note that, regardless of whether the seeds are popped or not, you can start your plants in starter cells or plastic cups that are filled with your grow medium – like soil or coco.

I love most about starter cells because they have everything you need to get your seeds to grow into seedlings with a medium that supports the proper growth of roots. If you have a humidity dome, you can easily propagate more than a single seedling at a time.

You may be thinking, "how do plastic cups work in this case?" Well, they work the same way only that in this case, you offer your seeds more room for root growth as opposed to the case of starter cells. This way, you get a chance to start your grow with larger plants. The most important thing is that you exercise caution not to allow the plants to grow too large in plastic cups as this might cause them to be root-bound, which is never good for young plants.

STARTING IN POTS, YOU WILL BE USING.

If you don't wish to pre-pop your seeds before transplanting them to their designated grow areas, you can place them directly into plant pots you intend to use for the plant's entire life.

While this will take the hassle of transplanting off your plate, the truth is that you stand the risk of overwhelming your plants with excess light and water than they need. On the other hand, if you choose to plant them directly into large pots, you must consider feeding them minimally and offering them light softly.

What if you choose to start with clones instead of seeds?

Remember, starting your marijuana plants from clones is a surefire way of ensuring that the plant genetics you are interested in growing is intact and precisely what you are looking for. With seeds, you risk growing your plants only to later realize that they are not the ones you wanted. While seeds can grow stronger than clones, the truth is that they can be a toss-up.

Your seeds can either be female or male, and even though they are the sex you are looking for, the truth is that you cannot guarantee they possess strain traits you are after. Clones, on the other hand, are derived from the plants you are looking for.

If you intend to replicate the genes to the tee, you must start from clones. Use a sterile scalpel and identify healthy fan leaves to cut from the branch at least at a 90° angle. Once you have the clippings, place them in water to avoid bubbles from entering the plant stem.

You can also use clipping gels on the clippings you took from the mother plants. Then insert the clones in starter cells and cover them with a humidity dome. Realize that standard starter cells are perfect for transplanting growing clones in coco or soil mediums. If you can, use Rockwool starter cells if you intend on using hydroponics as your grow medium because they are great for transplanting clones.

Ensure that the surroundings are humid enough – approximately 72-77º F – at least for two weeks. Once they get to the desired size, you are looking for, transplant following **these guidelines;**

8

TRANSPLANTING YOUR SEEDLINGS AND CLONES

Once you have your seedlings and clones as big as you would like them to be, you are ready for transplanting your marijuana plants into permanent pots for the rest of the life. One thing you must bear in mind is that marijuana plants hate jumping around from one bucket to the other. This is why it is necessary to keep transplanting to the minimum. The best way to do this is if you learn the appropriate pot size you wish the plants to end up in.

I will reiterate – keep transplanting to the minimum!

It should be between 1-2 transplants at most. Anything more than this might risk the plants suffering severe damage.

AVOIDING TRANSPLANT SHOCK

Have you ever taken a plant out of a container and put them on the ground or in another container?

When you move the plants from their original home to another, you expose them to a risk of deformation. Regardless of whether these deformations come in the form of limp, slow growth, dries up, or halted growth, these outcomes result from the direct consequences of extreme environmental changes.

The change here is – being uprooted!

Well, you might be thinking, "if transplanting damages the plant, what else can we do?"

Don't worry – just because your plants suffer transplant shock does not mean that they will eventually die. This means that you have to treat your seedlings like babies until they get back in shape. At this stage, they are very delicate, and depending on how severe the shock was will determine the length of recovery they will need before they spring back to normal.

To avoid shocking your plants too much during transplanting, try to pay attention to these directions;

Don't mess with the plant roots.

When transplanting, it is almost impossible not to disturb the roots. However, the most important thing you need to do here is to avoid digging into the plant area to lower the chances of damaging the plant roots. The best way to go about this is to try as much as you can to go around the entire medium and into the new pot by simply turning the pot or cell over as soon as the medium is compacted. This way, you can take the whole thing and move it into the new medium.

Avoid disturbing the root ball.

You must avoid shaking the soil or breaking the Rockwool in which your plants are in. This way, you ensure that the main root ball is intact.

Offer your plants plenty of water during transplanting.

Realize that nothing will shock your plants more than not giving it water. The truth is that when transplanting your plants, they will mostly be in recovery mode once they get out of the first medium. This is why you must ensure that when they need food, they can access it.

Ensure that the root balls are kept moist at all times. If not, the roots will dry and become damaged. Don't get me wrong – I am not saying that you should overwater your plants. Instead, you must watch them closely so that you can feed them when they need it.

KNOWING WHEN TO TRANSPLANT

This is one of the most important factors when it comes to transplanting. Yes, you may already know what transplanting is all about and what it is for, but if you don't know when to do it, then the chances are that your plants will live in their initial pots for eternity. When you cannot tell by just looking at the height of the plant, here are a few pointers on when the right to transplant comes;

Growing in starter cells

If your plants are in starter cells, simply feel around the root zone. If the medium is loose and there are not many roots, maintain them in their starter cells. However, if the medium is hardened around the root zone and the roots are good, then your plants are ready to get out of their initial home into the next.

Growing in soil

If you are growing your marijuana plants in large pots you wish to use for the rest of their life, then all you have to do is let your plants grow. However, if you started them in plastic cups with soil, ensure that your plants have rooted. The plants should not be root-bound if the soil is hardened but not compact, tip over the cup, and move the whole of it to a new bucket.

Growing in Rockwool cubes

It is important that the plant roots, in this case, are plentiful but not so few that transplanting will cause them damage. Rockwool is often used in coco and hydroponic mediums. In these two growth mediums, even a few roots would overload the plants with nutrients once transplanted.

PREPPING THE MEDIUM

Before getting your plants into the grow medium, ensure that it will not shock your plants any further. Well, this part is pretty easy if you are very careful. If you are planting them in soil, prepping the soil is easy because you need to add perlite to it and then gently water it. Then properly mix the elements very well to create super soil.

If you intend to plant them in coco coir, realize that the coco husks are neutral in pH. This means that you don't need to prep the medium other than breaking it down. This is usually in block form. Simply soak it and break it up and then fill a bucket with it. After that, soak the whole medium in the best nutrient solution of choice.

If you are using hydroponics, simply add a little seaweed extract into your medium. You could also add in shock treatment before you transplant your plants. Ensure that the temperature of both the water and nutrient solutions is at 68° F or room temperature. This ensures that you don't end up shocking the roots. Then load the water with a nutrient solution. Here are some of the best hydroponic mediums available for your indoor marijuana needs.

PREPPING NUTRIENTS

One more thing to go over before placing your plants in their permanent homes – the nutrient prep. How you mix your nutrients into your feeding solution is key to a successful transplant. This, too, is pretty easy. You must prep your water and mix all your nutrients and its elements well before you feed them to the plants.

Start by testing the pH and ppm levels of your water to ensure that they are optimal for healthy plants. If some reason your water is hard or feels too loaded with trace elements, simply run them through a reverse osmosis system to clean it up.

If you cannot use reverse osmosis systems, allow the water to sit out in open air for a while for the chlorine to be taken out. Aerate your water by hand or using a pump to ensure that there is sufficient oxygen for it to be beneficial to the plants.

Pay attention to the nutrients and the manufacturer's dosage recommendation. While some growers consider using half the recommended dosage by the manufacturer, you must base it on strength. Find the recommended dosage amount on the feeding chart that accompanied the nutrients. Then take the size of the reservoir or water canteen – if using soil or coco mediums – to determine how many mL of nutrients you will need.

Let us consider an example where your reservoir is 10 gallons – which roughly translates to about 38 liters – and your nutrients call for 5 mL of a given nutrient per gallon. In this case, you are going to mix 50 mL into your reservoir.

Now, if you wish to split the strength in half, you will use 25 mL of nutrients in the reservoir.

After, take the pH measurement of your new nutrient-rich water solution to ensure that it is optimal for your plants. Also, check the room temperature before you start feeding your plants.

9

GROW STAGE/VEGGING CYCLE

At this point, you have hung all the lights, calibrated, and checked the nutrients. The clones or seedlings are ready to transplant. All there is left to be done here is to get your marijuana plants to their permanent home for them to get started with the vegging stage.

You may be wondering, "what is the vegging stage of plant growth?"

The vegging stage is also referred to as the vegetative stage of plant growth. One thing you must note about the vegging cycle is that your plant life is actively growing, and its structure is being formed.

The fan leaves are growing bigger, the branches are getting stronger, and the root zones are expanding to future flowering sites. In short, the plant is creating the structure it needs for it to live, grow, and get the harvest you are looking for.

Here are three major things the vegetative cycle does;

Creation of root growth for total plant nutrition

If your marijuana plant lacks adequate roots, the chances are that they will not get the nutrition they need with the efficiency requires. Realize that plants require lots of roots for them to absorb the nutrient elements they need out of their grow medium – whether soil, coco coir, or hydroponics.

Foliage growth to absorb light.

Plants need an adequate amount of light to support the various vital processes of feeding and growth. They take in CO2 through the leaves for them to eat, grow, and breathe – and this is where the leaves are supposed to grow well for these functions to take place.

You can also get fertilizer boosters here to improve foliage growth;

Stems and branches

For the leaves and flowering sites to be present, they must have a place to grow, which is the role of the branches. When the branches are strong enough, they will lead to the growth of more leaves and flowering sites. Additionally, they will promote the growth of big buds on the plants as long as they need to be ahead of the harvest time.

HOW TO TRANSPLANT THOSE SEEDLINGS AND CLONES

Now, you know what the vegging stage is, and the next thing is to get started on transplanting your seedlings or clones into large buckets/permanent home.

The first thing is for you to check your plants and their cells to ensure that they are ready to transplant. If you are using perlite starter cells or soil in plastic cups, it is important to ensure that the medium is hardened and has lots of roots. This usually takes between 1-2 weeks. If using Rockwool, on the other hand, allow the seedlings or clones to produce as many roots as possible first. Ensure that they are completely soaked throughout the day because if it dries out, the roots will, too, is not a good thing. This, too, takes about 1-2 weeks.

Additionally, the light mustn't overpower the plants. For instance, if you are growing your marijuana plants with a light of 200 watts, you must ensure that you dimmed it so that the light does not overpower the plants.

Once you know that the plants are ready for transplanting, then get right to it.

Transplanting in to hydro

One of the greatest advantages of transplanting into hydro systems is that you don't have to worry about bigger buckets. Here, the DWC bucket in the reservoir they grow in will be enough to hold your plant roots throughout their life. In short, hydro systems allow you to simply transplant into the grow medium directly, and you are ready to grow!

Transplanting into pebbles

This is also referred to as the drip, DWC, or ebb and flow system. The first thing here is to ensure that you soak the pebbles at least for 8-24 hours before using it with an air stone. This ensures that they expand.

The next thing is to measure out the size of the basket needed for use. Fill it with pebbles until a quarter way. If you are using Rockwool, you can transplant young plants directly into the baskets with the pebbles. If using foam cells and the roots are below the cells, cut the cells off, and then transplant them directly into the grow medium. Ensure that the pebbles are filled ¼ way too.

What if you are working with starter cells?

Well, in that case, plant them directly into the pebbles as usual. However, ensure that you keep an eye on the water for the perlite or peet to wash away. It is important that they completely wash off the plant, off the pebbles, and out of the reservoir as you change your feedings.

Transplanting rockwool into rockwool

When transplanting your marijuana seedlings or clones, you can go from Rockwool cubes to larger Rockwool cubes to get a complex network of strong roots. You can do it in flood trays. You must note that when doing Rockwool-to-Rockwool transplants, you must continue vigorous root growth just like when they were young.

In other words, start by carving out holes the size and shape of Rockwool you are using in the new Rockwool cube or trays. Then soak the cubes or trays in the preferred feeding strength at a water pH of between 5.5 and 6.0. Allow the nutrient solution to drain off completely. Then insert the cubes with your clones into the larger trays or cubes. Ensure that the roots are headed downwards.

Transplanting in a loose medium such as coco coir or soil

When going from Rockwool or cell into such mediums as soil or coco coir, it can be quite challenging. This is why you must exercise extra caution when handling the plant roots. You must never overfeed your plants.

Simply start by using at least a gallon or two pots. If you use pots that are too big, you risk overwatering your plants. The best thing is to fill the pots about an inch above the tip and then tap the medium to ensure that it settles down more. This ensures that any air pockets that form in the medium are taken out hence creating a "fill line" you must not go over when watering.

Once your grow medium is ready, make a hole in it – the size of your starter cells or Rockwool trays/cubes – for transplanting. Now, you are ready to plant your young marijuana plants in the medium. Then cover the cells completely with coco or soil. However, if using Rockwool cubes, ensure that you cover the cube completely to only expose the top of the cube. Finally, water your medium and expose your plants to light.

That said, realize that soil tends to take in water and to leave the Rockwool cubes to dry. You should frequently check your medium and Rockwool cubes to ensure that they are saturated as required.

To reiterate, if using nutrient-rich soil, it is not necessary to add more nutrients to your feeding schedule. This is especially the case because everything your plants need is already available to them – and then some!

There is no need for supplemental nutrients in soil-grown marijuana plants.

VEG: WEEK 1

This week is slightly different from all the others, depending on whether you are starting with marijuana seedlings or clones. This will determine the kind of nutrient mix you will use.

If you are growing on soil, you will likely water your plants twice a week. The first watering is with the nutrient mix, and the second watering is with plain water at a pH of 6.8. when growing your plants in soil, it is necessary to feed every watering. This **watering guide** will help you get it right;

If you are transplanting your plants to the hydro system, pay attention to the pH levels during the first week by following these **guidelines;**

There is a high likelihood that they will become acidic with time. Because your plants are still young, this fluctuation will not be drastic. However, you must cultivate the habit of checking the pH every day to ensure consistency.

Ensure that you pay attention to the PPM levels – between 200 and 250 for seedlings and 550-700 for clones – during the first week.

That said, test the pH every other day and top it with fresh water to maintain acceptable levels of your plants. Additionally, the lights should be no more than 24 inches above your tallest plants and no closer than 18 inches.

VEG: WEEK 2

During the second week, your plants are taller. This means that you must adjust the lighting to ensure that you maintain the 18-24 inches height of the plant canopy.

If your plants are in the soil, you must ensure that the nutrient strength you feed it with is at least ¼ strength in the feeding schedule. This is mainly because the forest soil is amended with nutrients already. The last thing you want here is to overfeed your plants and cause nutrient burns.

As the nutrients naturally get depleted in the soil, you can gradually increase the dosage over the coming weeks until you attain a full nutrient strength suitable for the optimal growth of your plants. Realize that some soil does not need supplemental nutrients – at least until the flowering stage. If working with soil, ensure that you use water with your soil.

However, if you are using a hydro system for your plants, this is the time to drain and refill your reservoirs for plant feeding. You must do this every week until harvest time – you better get used to it! Every week, you will drain the reservoir, refill it with RO water, add nutrients, check the PPM, and adjust the pH as required.

During this week, you must start pruning and training your plants.

Pruning and training your plants

This should be done around day ten of transplanting your seedlings or clones. While it is unnecessary to take many leaves off the plant this early, there are long-term benefits to pruning and training marijuana plants at this point.

These benefits include;

- It creates more foliage for your plants, enabling them to capture more light. More light is a good thing as far as plant growth is concerned.
- Pruning allows the plants to grow directly towards the buds during the flowering stage.
- Training allows plants to access more light, which stimulates the growth of flower sites
- Training maximizes the light coverage across the plant canopy for better, even, and controlled growth.
- Training controls the plant shape and height hence maximizing space in the growing area.

Topping & FIM'ing plants

You may be wondering, "what is the purpose of topping the plants, anyway?"

Well, topping plays a significant role in stimulating the growth of more shots from the main shoot at the top of the plant simply by cutting off the topmost plant shoot. This allows the growth of two new sets of leaves with new shoots, hence promoting more leaves and bud sites.

Topping goes a long way in training your plants to grow shorter than they normally do. This may or may not be a good thing depending on how you would like your plants to grow.

FIM'ing, on the other hand, plays an important role in helping the formation of more buds on the plants. To get even bigger buds,

When you get rid of 2/3's of the tallest growing plant shoots – at the leaves and not the stem – you simply create at least four times more bud sites when your plants begin flowering.

Be careful not to cut too much as this might only lead to 2x bud sites.

FIM'ing, in itself, helps your plants grow wider and shorter than they normally would.

Low-stress training

This is another important technique that yields similar results as topping as far as plants are exposed to more light than usual. This, in turn, promotes more foliage and formation of more bud sites.

Using a light string, gently tie the plant branches to the sides of the growing pots – especially when using fabric pots. If not, you can simply drill a hole in the plastic. If you can bend the main stem and tie, feel free to do so. Otherwise, you can bend the branches down – that works fine too. This way, your plants will focus more on growing stronger and vigorous instead of directing their energy to the main cola.

The good thing is that you can use thing technique to top for more vigorous growth. Remember, when you take parts of the plant away, it takes time for your plant to get back on track. It is your choice to consider one or the other to achieve your goals.

Sea of Green

Perhaps you have heard of big harvests using this technique – and that is true!

If you do it correctly, the sea of green will help your plants create large canopies for light, hence achieving bigger buds and many of them, for that matter. If you want SOG, it is advisable to have at least four plants. That said, your plants must note be crowded in the growing space at all.

Begin with low-stress training so that your plants can grow wide and not too tall – considering SOG is all about wide coverage. Then lay trellis netting above plants to allow them to keep spreading and limit the canopy height. As your plants continue to grow, ensure to "lolly-pop" prune them. This is simply pruning them for new growth on the main branches and other vital parts that support the growth of flowering sites. This must be done well, especially during the flowering stage.

VEG: WEEK 3

If you are planting your plants in soil, it is necessary to provide at least ½ strength of nutrients in the feeding schedule – especially when using Fox Farm Ocean Forest Soil or any other soil that is not super soil.

Bear in mind that as the nutrients in the soil get depleted naturally, you must increase the dosage over the coming weeks until you achieve full strength of nutrients that is optimal for your plants.

If you are planting them in hydroponic systems, this is the time to drain and refill your reservoirs. Simply drain the reservoirs, refill them with RO water, add in nutrients, check the PPM, and finally adjust the pH.

Nutrient lock and nutrient issues

During the third week of vegging, you must take time to go over all nutrient issues. Most specifically, check the nutrient lock. If your marijuana plants have been growing just fine and then you realize that they are beginning to wilt or brown at the tips, there is a high chance that they are suffering nutrient lockout.

Some of the causes of this are overwatering – especially in coco and soil. However, in hydroponic systems, it could be caused by mixing in too many nutrients – especially a dose that is too strong for your plants. The simplest way to correct this is to flush your plants and get the nutrient feeding schedule gradually on track this way.

But what if your plants are not wilting or browning and instead yellowing and losing their green color?

In this case, there is a high chance that the soil and nutrients used do not have all the elements your plants need. To correct this, simply give your plants the nutrients they are missing!

Pest control and fungal infections

If you notice that your plants are changing color to brown or yellow and that they have holes or burn marks on the leaves, there is a high chance of pest or fungal infections. Considering that the nutrients and surrounding conditions are stable for the plant, this issue can be difficult to spot. That is why you must keep a close eye on your plants at all times for even the slightest change in their morphological traits.

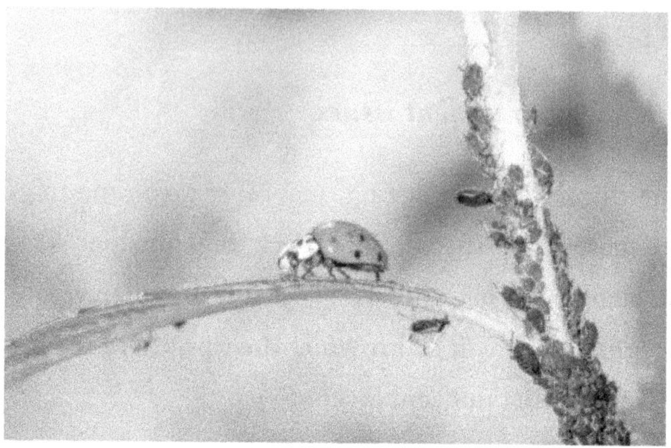

Pests are indeed visible on plants, be it holes or trails on the leaves. If you notice even a slight possibility that your plants are sick, the first thing you must do is inspect them. If you find pests on them, use natural pesticides to get rid of them. You could try natural soap and water as that kills bugs chomping at your plants.

Neem oil, on the other hand, will help kill spider mites. If you like, you can use natural predators – like mantises and ladybugs – to help kill bugs without necessarily rinsing off your plants.

Understand that fungal and bacterial infections often cause rotting of roots and eventually buds. If you find this out early enough, it is easy to spray them off and ensure that you keep them away using water, neem oil, or milk. You can also give your plant vitamins so that they can try to heal themselves fast. However, if the plant is too far along in an infection, get rid of it before it can infect other plants.

Synthetic versus Biological Pest Control

Management of pests is essential, no matter if you choose to go synthetic or biological. Synthetic insecticide resolutions will play a key role in keeping your plants protected from the damage that pests can create. However, they also pose a risk to other animals in your environment. And the pests will learn to develop a resistance to these synthetic measures, and they will come back with a vengeance.

On the other hand, if you want to keep your plants as organic as possible, there are also some potent biological solutions you can integrate to produce good results. These natural pesticides are non-toxic to wildlife, beneficial insects, pets, and humans, and they are less likely for the pest to build resistance. Another benefit is they break down quickly, so they have a low impact on your grow environment.

Basic Insect Control

The easiest way to ensure that bugs and pests will not infiltrate your cannabis plants is to use healthy, fertile soil. Also, controlling the environment through proper lighting levels, ventilation, and keeping your plants watered and appropriately drained will help keep the pests at bay. Be sure to keep a daily look on your plants, make sure they are clean from debris and pests, and keep them happy in a healthy environment. By doing it, you will get to the end of the season with the least amount of issues.

Aphid

Aphids are parasitic aphids (or aphids) that form a sub-family within the order of hemipteran insects. Like many other insects, it can represent a severe pest in the numerous plant species on which it feeds (nutrient plant), as well as being a vector insect of various viruses and diseases.

These are small insects of different colors (usually yellow, black, or green) with a size of 1 to 3 mm. Its body is ovoidal, and the three parts that make it up (head, thorax, and abdomen) cannot be distinguished. They may lack wings (wingless) or have two pairs of small, transparent membranous wings. In the final part of the abdomen, they have two small appendages that serve to secrete repellent substances for their natural predators.

They are usually found on the underside of leaves and stems, forming large colonies of dozens (or hundreds) of individuals. They develop a symbiotic relationship with other insects, such as ants or bees. Aphids secrete a substance sweetened by the anus, which protects the aphids from their predators. Something similar happens with bees, which incorporate these molasses to the honey they produce.

Aphids may need a single plant to complete their biological cycle, called monocyclic cycle, or may need two different plants, then the dioic cycle. They can also reproduce through eggs (sexual reproduction, females, and males intervene, which tend to be smaller) or asexual (parthenogenesis). Its propagation is curious because as the generations progress and depending on environmental factors are given different forms in the offspring, thus providing a vast degree of polymorphism. The metamorphosis experienced by the nymphs until the adult stage is minimal so that larvae and adults bear a considerable resemblance except, of course, in its size.

Whitefly

Whiteflies are homopterous insects of the Aleurodidae family (Aleyrodidae) that attack many types of cultivated plants, including cannabis plants. These are small mosquitoes with a 2mm long and whitish appearance, with a pair of wings that serve as a movement method. Their usual location is on the underside of the leaves (where they also lay the eggs, as we will see later), and, like other sucking insects such as aphids or woodlice, they feed by sucking the sap from the plants.

A whitefly body is divided into three zones: head thorax and abdomen. Like other insects, it has six legs and also a pair of white wings as a locomotion system. As we have said, it has a biting-sucking mouthpiece, thanks to which it can feed on the sap of leaves and young tissues.

This insect lays and fertilizes eggs, which it deposits on the underside of the leaves in an amount of 180-200 per laying. These eggs are almost microscopic, oval-pyramidal, and have a yellowish-white color. They normally have four generations a year (one generation is the duration of the life cycle of the insect, from the time they lay the eggs until the adult dies) depending on the climatic and hygienic conditions. However, in the greenhouse, they can reach ten generations a year, thus becoming a severe plague.

We can easily see that a greenhouse or a grow space will become its favorite habitat, as it is a plague that likes high temperatures and relatively humid atmospheres, being then the summer its ideal time.

From the egg-laying to the birth of the larva, approximately 24 hours pass; then, it will take another four weeks for the larva to become an adult, passing through 4 instars or larval-nymphalid stages, with scale form and located on the underside of the leaves.

We can alternate our plants with others, creating an association of beneficial plants with each other; In this case, cultivating marigolds, Chinese carnations, or basil will help prevent the appearance of whitefly, as its smell repels them. We should check the back of the leaves regularly for adults or larvae, and use every few days a biological insecticide such as potassium soap or neem oil. Using yellow insect-trapping tapes, where adults will be stuck, will make things more difficult for these insects.

Caterpillars

During the outdoor marijuana growing season, many insects feed on our marijuana plants. In this case, we need to consider one of the most voracious predators that attack cannabis plants, leaving them destroyed and useless for their consumption, the caterpillars.

Caterpillars are the larvae of the Lepidoptera family's insects, better known after their metamorphosis as beautiful butterflies. Many species of butterflies are found around the world. There are many different types of caterpillars, with variable colors and sizes, but, yes, they all have precise characteristics in common, such as the segmented body, the six legs or the hooks of the pseudo path.

Before finding a caterpillar in our marijuana plants, we will see how the butterflies rest on the buds or leaves, generally in the highest parts where there are the most extensive and unreachable buds. The butterfly will deposit its eggs typically before the winter season arrives, these eggs will be born when the environmental temperatures are the most adequate, needing the heat of the end of summer which coincides with the arrival of winter two months away. It is feasible that the butterflies deposit their eggs, which are not born until there are suitable conditions for their development.

The caterpillars are long-bodied insects, divided into segments with varied colors, generally adapted to camouflage among the vegetation to avoid being devoured by birds or other natural predators of these insects. They move through its six main legs next to the 10 "false" legs distributed along its body, which can vary in position according to the type of caterpillar in question.

These voracious predators of green matter do not breathe through the mouth but do so through small holes distributed along the body, called spiracles. These holes lead to a network of internal tubes or tracheas that connect, providing oxygen directly to the cells, being a very active and spectacular respiratory system.

After doing the exhaustive search in our plants, we should do what we should do if we have detected a caterpillar or observe plants in bitten buds, to apply a product that repels or kills the eggs and larvae of butterflies.

Recommendations for a crop free of caterpillars:

- Divide the butterflies sitting on the plants.
- Look for the eggs in the leaves.
- During flowering, check the buds for signs of bites.
- In case of detection, apply a product compatible with the caterpillars.
- Stop applying the product within the last 15 days (before harvesting).
- Check the plants and buds after harvest and remove the infected or bitten parts.
- Collect the caterpillars that are born in the case of not being able to apply the product.

Thrips

Trips or Thysanoptera are a widespread problem faced by many marijuana growers. It is a tiny plague that sucks the sap from the plants of your crop. There are different species of thrips. They can be tiny winged insects (that measure millimeters) or have the appearance of small pale worms.

Regardless of the species, thrips are a nightmare for growers around the world. They can reproduce up to 12 times per year. Once they mature, they survive flying from plant to plant. Apart from cannabis, the favorite crop of thrips seems to be cotton, although they can attack many other types of plants. But they love marijuana. And when they appear in the early stages of cultivation, they are incredibly harmful.

The best way to get rid of thrips is to prevent an infestation from occurring. Make sure you disinfect the growing space entirely before you start cultivating, not only keeping the place clean but also eliminating any dead plant material.

Once you have started your crop, hang anti-insect adhesive strips. Like flypaper, they will trap most of the flying insects around them, which will stick to them. Finishing thrips once they have made an appearance is the only way to save a crop and prevent a new infestation. The best methods (without aggressive chemicals) are potassium soap and neem oil.

Fungi

If you happen to see any issues that arise with scabs, blotches, mold, or rusty leaves, you have a problem with fungi disease of your cannabis plants. One common way to combat these diseases is through the use of copper and sulfur.

Copper is the best option before you notice the infection or immediately after you notice the effects. You can get these in a liquid or powder form. You need to use the copper over the entire plant each day for seven to ten days until you see the effects wearing off of your plants.

The sulfur fungicide is as effective as the copper solution; however, it is not wise to apply this medium if you have high temperatures at your grow location as it may result in the burning of your plants.

Powdery Mildew

The Mildew is a cryptogamic fungus disease that results in fungal hyphae in plant tissues, wood, leather, paper, etc. Relatively similar to the Oidium, the Mildew delves into the tissues of leaves, stems, and fruits and not only remains on the surface as does the first. Being an endoparasite, we will not appreciate its structure until the damages produced in the plant are considerable, injuries that are visible in the aerial parts of the plants.

This fungus is part of the family of Peronosporaceae, which includes seven genera and about 600 species.

In agriculture, it usually damages potato, vine, tobacco, and Cucurbitaceae crops, without forgetting, of course, cannabis. It is quite a specific pathogen because each species attacks a particular - and relatively small - number of plants. One of the most well-known species is the Plasmopara viticola or Mildew of the vine, which was introduced in Europe in 1878 by the French when importing vine stocks resistant to the phylloxera, but host of this fungus.

As preventive treatments, we can choose sprays with;

Chamomile broth - 50 g of flowers per liter of water dissolved at a rate of 9 liters of water for each liter of preparation

Garlic - an infusion of 50g of garlic cloves per liter of water dissolved in a 1 liter of preparation

Bordelés broth, copper oxychloride, and dithiocarbamates are also frequently used as prevention.

Fusarium

Fusarium is the pathogen that causes Fusarium head blight (FHB) of wheat and other cereals.

Fusarium is the name given to a genus of filamentous fungi that live in the soil, in association with all plants, including marijuana. Most species are saprophytic, that is, they feed on waste from other organisms. Fusariosis is the name given to the disease caused by certain plant species of Fusarium fungi (phytopathogenic), which develop here as parasites.

They are a severe contamination agent in laboratories, and some Fusarium species attack cereals and produce mycotoxins capable of affecting humans, producing diseases such as Keratomycosis, Onychomycosis, or Panama disease, in addition to causing various types of skin infections.

Unfortunately, there is no valid or fungicidal treatment for infected Fusarium plants. Therefore, prevention is the best and the only option we have to avoid fusarium; we must be very conscientious with the hygiene in our culture, disinfecting clippers, irrigation tanks, sherds, etc. using them. We must start from a quality substrate, with known properties.

Step by step instructions to Prevent Cannabis Root Rot

You can reduce your odds of root spoil by taking a couple of precaution measures:

Have sound soil with the valuable organism and microorganisms' populaces. These populaces help keep the organism answerable for root spoil leveled out.

Water your plants effectively. This implies estimating the measure of water given to each plant and watching every day how they react to the measure of water given. It is smarter to see a plant start to shrink than to overwater during this procedure.

Have breathable soil. Growing in savvy pots and adding perlite to the dirt are two ways to help encourage the oxygen stream and enable the dirt to deplete appropriately.

The fine buildup is a typical sickness that appears on the leaves and buds of cannabis plants. At first, you will discover it on the lower parts of a plant where there is less sun introduction, wind stream, and more significant levels of mugginess. This kind of mold shows up as a white powder that sits on the outside of the leaves. When it shows up, it spreads quickly and can rapidly advance onto bud locales. Luckily, because the fine buildup is so unmistakable, it's uncommon for a plant to bite the dust from it. The fundamental concern is it renders the item unfit available to be purchased.

An effective method to Prevent Powdery Mildew on Cannabis

It's normal for cultivators to take a protection course with fine mold. Here are some best practices you should seriously think about:

- Splash your plants with natural items and fungicides
- Prune your plants to expand wind current

- Splash fertilizer tea or arrangements with differing PH levels to upset the spread of the infection
- Focus on which hereditary qualities are helpless to fine buildup and think about concentrating on different strains

If your nursery becomes contaminated with fine mold, there is an approach to expel it by showering the collected cannabis in an H2O2/H2O arrangement. By blending a modest quantity of 3% hydrogen peroxide (H2O2) with water, you make an answer that disinfects the collected plants and evacuates the buildup. This is a meticulous procedure, yet it can spare you from a tainted yield.

What Is Leaf Septoria?

Leaf septoria is a brutal looking malady that shows into first on the lower branches and makes leaves scab and yellow. It uncovered itself throughout the late spring when high temperatures joined with summer downpours or dampness from watering leave the foliage clammy. Nitrogen lacks can likewise fill in as an impetus to the sickness.

Even though leaf septoria won't slaughter your plants, it will decrease yields. When you see the disease, it's imperative to evacuate and discard the departs. Abstain from placing the tainted material in your manure heap to forestall future episodes. Showering plants with Bacillus subtilis fungicides can likewise help moderate the spread of the sickness.

Step by step instructions to Prevent Leaf Septoria on Cannabis

To counter the effect of this episode, there are a couple of moves you can make:

- You should have a perfect nursery space with sound soils. This is the most significant precaution measure you can take. If you have a flare-up, you may need to supplant your growing medium before planting once more.
- Tidy up your whole grow room, particularly if you're working an indoor nursery.
- Use trickle lines to water your plants, so the leaves don't get wet.
- Space the plants further separated to keep coordinating dampness off the plants and the moistness levels down.

Root decay, fine mold, and leaf septoria are only a couple of the more typical ailments that can appear on cannabis plants. Different maladies incorporate the TMV (tobacco mosaic infection), fusarium, and verticillium wither. These illnesses have a typical topic when it comes to controlling: anticipation. Plant specialists must furnish plants with the correct supplements, microscopic organisms, and microorganisms to be prepared to deal with contaminations for similar reasons we as people eat well and exercise to forestall disease.

Hereditary qualities assume a significant job in directing how crippling an ailment can be to a plant. Watch your nursery, see patterns with specific hereditary qualities, and stick to solid matured hereditary qualities that are steady.

At this point, you must prune your plants further. It does not matter whether you are training them or not. What matters is that you prune to strengthen their branches to receive more light by getting rid of the lower hanging or even poor-performing growths. This will, in turn, redirect the light received through the leaves.

Bear in mind that leaves take in light. Therefore, if you get rid of too much foliage, you risk stunting the plants because they will not receive optimal light for their growth. That said, if your plants are damaged, they will try as much as they can to recover from injuries. However, if you prune them too much, you will shock them and hinder their growth. This is mainly because most of their energy will be diverted into recovery instead of strengthening the bud-producing branches.

VEG: WEEK 4/PRE-FLOWERING

How do you know that your plants are ready for flowering?

By the fourth week, your plants should be naturally ready for flowering. This is the time when they also start showing their sex.

For instance, if it is male cannabis, you can tell by their pollen sacs growing in between the nodes. If female cannabis, they grow white pestles in between the nodes.

It is necessary that at this stage, you ensure that you do a week-long flush of your plants – especially when beginning to show their sexes. This way, they are ready for flowering nutrients. If you wish not to flush your plants, you can give your soil plants more nutrients. If they are hydroponic, drain and refill the reservoirs with RO water. Then add in nutrients if you wish not to flush. Otherwise, you can use reverse osmosis machines to clean the water. Check the PPM and aim at keeping it between 0 and 50 PPM. Ensure that you also adjust the pH.

On the last day of the vegetative stage, allow your plants a 24-hour exposure to darkness and then a 12-hour light and 12-hour off cycle.

Think about it, when you do a 12/12 light cycle, it triggers flowering. Why is that? You may be wondering how that change in light exposure is possibly vital to plant growth? Well, it turns out that light is a big deal as far as vegging and flowering.

According to research, plants have been shown to possess a gene called Phytochrome Far Red (PFR), which tells plants to keep vegging. When you suddenly expose the plants to darkness, the gene changes to Phytochrome red, which is non-active. Therefore, darkness for at least 12 hours causes the PFR gene to be "switched off" to allow the plants to start flowering.

That said, you must bear in mind that when your plants are not exposed to light at all, that stands in the way of growth. While it is necessary to go all-dark before getting into the flowering stage, you must not overdo it. You cannot expose your plants to 36 hours of darkness because that is extreme.

So, what happens when a door opens, or a light leak comes through a hole in your grow tent? While this poses a problem during the vegging cycle, it is harmful to the flowering stage. If your plants are supposed to be in darkness but light leaks through, it will trigger activation of the PFR gene, which, over time, sends your plants back to vegging.

When this happens, simply take back your plants into the vegging cycle and repeat putting them on 24-36 hours of darkness period for at least 2-3 days.

During the pre-flowering period, do the light cycles as follows;

Day 22-27, schedule lights on and off for 18/6 hours

Day 28, schedule 18/24 lights on/off cycles.

When the light is on, you must water and feed your plants as required. When the lights are off, allow your MH lights to cool down before you can switch the bulbs out to HPS. Turn off the timers to allow the plants to be in the dark for no less than 24 hours.

Remember that this is the last week of veg. The most important thing is that you pay attention to all the tips necessary in ensuring your plant's transition well from vegging to flowering. If you don't do it correctly, you risk delaying the flowering stage, resulting in delayed harvest periods.

That said, the best way your plants can grow is by taking clippings/cuts from the mother plant. While it is challenging to clone from a flowering plant, the clippings will take time to look as they should. Different genes are activated during the flowering stage as opposed to the vegging stage.

10

FLOWERING STAGE/BLOOM CYCLE

All the growth your plants have achieved since the very first day was leading up to the flowering stage. This is the stage when you will see flowers emerge. The buds will also swell before harvest time.

One thing you must note is that flowering properly is critical. If done the wrong way, the chances are to set you back to between 2-30 days. This is why you must pay very close attention to your marijuana plants and correct any issues that might arise along the way to ensure that they grow properly.

WHAT IS THE FLOWERING STAGE?

Note that the flowering stage often marks the end of vegging and growth of your plants' lives. It also marks the beginning of flowering that eventually produce buds you are looking for. Because of this, it is the most important stage of your plant's life.

The flowering stage is necessary for the propagation of your plants, considering this is when the pollens are released and received by the flowers to yield seeds. If the female plants are left alone, there is a chance that they will continue to grow their buds and flowers until harvest time.

From the first week through to the third week of flowering, your plants will continue stretching until they meet their peak height – otherwise referred to as the *"flower stretch."*

The lighting here is supposed to be 12 hours on and 12 hours off. This ensures that your plants get adequate exposure to darkness for the PFR gene to remain active and keep your plants to veg even more. Bear in mind that the temperatures required for flowering should be 10 degrees less than the vegging temperature. The humidity is bound to reduce as well.

MIXING NUTRIENTS FOR PLANTS

As we have already mentioned before, this stage of flowering starts when you mix the nutrients required for flowering is integrated into the feeding schedule – if you have not done that already.

As soon as you start mixing nutrients into the soil, the concentration must be half the required strength. Ensure that you add nutrients to water every 2-3 feedings. If using hydroponic systems or coco mediums, be sure to use nutrients right from the start and keep using them as they have been used.

FLOWER: WEEK 1

Here, we are going to reset the days from day 29 to day 1. You may be wondering, "why is the flowering stage counted from the start?"

This is mainly because the vegging stage may take another 1-2 weeks for certain plants – including marijuana.

What lighting system are you using? Well, if you are using HID grow lights and have now switched to HPS bulbs, you are on the right track. If not, then this is the time to do so. You must ensure that your lighting schedule is switched to 12 hours on and 12 hours off to help your plant's circadian rhythm to start blooming.

What you will note differently on the environment chart in the flowering stage is that the growing space should be kept cooler and with a dryer humidity.

Plant maintenance

This is where you put up your Trellis Netting if your plants are growing too tall. As the plants start the stretching process – which will keep happening here – during the first month of flowering, your trellis net will go a long way in helping your plants maintain an even canopy. This ensures that the lighting distribution is even too.

If you realize that some plant branches are getting too tall, you must feed them through the trellis net. This will allow other branches to achieve a similar height.

The soil from this point going forward requires that you increase the watering frequency, considering your plants have become taller, and the roots are even larger. This means that the plants have a higher feeding capacity.

That said, ensure that you maintain the intervals of feeding and watering to prevent nutrient locks or salt build-ups. If you are not using super soils, then ensure that you use nutrients in all your feedings from now on. Ensure that ½ to full strength is used.

If using a hydroponic system, ensure that you drain and refill the reservoirs with RO water. Add in the nutrients, check the PPM, and adjust the pH.

Pruning and Trimming During the Flowering Stretch

At this point, it is necessary and recommended that the small branches and leaves are pruned off. This should be done at the lower one-third of the plants in your grow room. Here is why;

Increase breathability

Flowering plants like marijuana often produce more moisture in the grow room/tent environment. To prevent airborne diseases – like molds, pests, and powdery mildew – ensure that you cut down on the foliage and allow fain air to move freely through the garden.

Higher yields

Now, the remainder top two-thirds of the plants are supposed to receive more light considering this is where the majority of your harvest and high-quality buds and flowers will be produced. Realize that the lower third of your plant is too shaded from branches and leaves above. In other words, they take up energy from your plants to maintain the branches and leaves. If you were to get rid of them completely, then the plant will be forced to redistribute its energy equal to the parts getting most of its beneficial lighting.

FLOWER: WEEK 2

This is the week that marks the halfway point of your plant's growing cycle. At this point, the schedule should be your second nature. During this week, you will do the last pruning of your plants.

If growing in soil, your watering will get even more frequent as your plants become even taller and the roots larger. In other words, your plants have achieved an even higher feeding capacity. You must maintain the feeding and watering intervals of your plants to prevent salt build-up and nutrient locks from happening.

If growing in hydroponic systems, the usual is required. Simply drain the reservoir and refill it with RO water. Add in nutrients, check the PPM, and finally adjust the pH.

Maintain the pruning level you desire

Just to reiterate, this is the last week to make essential pruning maintenance of your plants before they can flower. Trimming and pruning your marijuana plants can be very stressful for your plants. Therefore, it is necessary and important that you do this task before your plants start using buds and flowers for 100% of their time.

Realize that any mass pruning at this point might greatly and negatively impact your final harvest and quantity of yields. If you have a few more branches and leaves, ensure that you cut them down at this point,

Here are two caveats to that;

The truth is, your plants will focus on the growth of flowers. Any new growth at the bottom of the plant should be trimmed. This allows all of its energy to go into the production of bud sites and flowers.

Look around your plants for any signs of yellowing leaves or even damaged/broken stems to get rid of them. If these damages are not removed early enough, your plants will focus their energy on repairing the damaged parts instead of focusing on flowering and budding.

That said, this is the stage when your plant's sex should be seen. If you cannot see your plants' sex, it might be time to go back to vegging.

You must know what sex you are working with – whether male or female. If the sex does not show by the second week of flowering, you will have to reveg your plants. This is done by simply switching their light cycles back to 16/8 hours or 24/0 hours.

But what if you can already see the sex of the plants?

In that case, this is what you must do with your newly identified plants;

Are you looking to breed your plants? At this point, the leave plants as they are and the pollen sacs will burst during the second or third week of flowering. In that case, if you only want females, you must immediately get rid of all male plants. This is mainly because even the smallest bit of pollen is enough to stimulate seed growth in your plants.

If you are not sure what you wish to do, the safest trick is to separate males from females. Separating them from each other ensures that you collect the pollen sacs from all your male plants and put them in glass jars for freezing – for later use.

Then you can work with the females and maintain them all the way to harvest time.

Pest control

While we have talked about pest control before, you must understand pest prevention, regulation, and eradication. You must keep this list in mind even before you start growing your cannabis plants;

Cleanliness

Ensure that you sterilize your growing areas and equipment. You must wear protective clothing but also make sure that they were not exposed to anything outside the growing area.

Prevention

Ensure that you have neem oil in the growing area to use it as a way of preventing pest infestation from happening in the first place. Neem oil has been known to sterilize spider mites and other soft-bodied insects from reproducing.

When the buds start growing, you must be more meticulous with plant care. If you suspect that your plants are attractive to pests and that the flowers and scents going on are going to attract pests from all over, ensure that you spray neem oil to protect them from pest infestation.

Unlike pest control during the vegging stage, there are several caveats when it comes to pest control during the flowering stage. Here, it is preferable to use natural predators. This ensures that unwanted chemicals do not get into buds.

If you used chemicals before, try to keep off using them during this stage. The truth is that pesticides can leach into the buds and the growing medium in use. Once they are soaked and absorbed by the roots, they are hard to get flush from the plant.

FLOWER: WEEK 3

If you have not noticed, there is a chance that your plants will have stretched and grown significantly over the past three weeks compared to the first four weeks of vegging – and that is normal!

This is often referred to as the stretching period. Though it is temporary, the plants will finish stretching soon and start converting most of their energy into flowering and the swelling of buds, at least for the remainder of their growth.

There is nothing to worry about as long as you ensure the grow room is not leaking light in. Ensure that you keep a close eye on the PPM levels and the pH. As long as they are maintained at optimal levels, you are good.

If you are growing your marijuana plants in soil mediums, ensure that you maintain internals of watering and feeding to prevent salt build-up and nutrient lock. If using the hydro system, ensure that you drain and refill the reservoirs with RO water. Then add in nutrients required, check the PPM levels, and adjust the pH as required.

FLOWER: WEEK 4

At this point, you will see your flowers begin to plump up. The buds will also begin to ripen a little with the hairs coming up out of them. The aromas will become stronger and stronger by the day.

If you notice clusters of white salt rocks in the soil, there is a concentration of nutrients that have not been used up trying to mess around with your plants. At this point, you are roughly halfway through the flowering stage, which is a good time to flush.

You may be wondering, "what is flushing, and why should it be done this close to the harvest time?"

Well, flushing simply refers to the process of purging through the current growing medium to ensure that the plants get rid of salt build-up and excess nutrients they do not need. This way, the plants achieve a fresh balance of nutrients and water. The salt concentrations, pH, and PPM levels will fluctuate, causing adverse effects on the plants.

In using a hydroponic system, flushing your plants will help clean the plant pots or buckets, dissolve salts in the mediums, tubes, reservoirs, and pumps. To make this happen, drain the system of all nutrient-rich water and replace all that with RO water.

If you are planting in soil mediums, flushing ensures that there is no salt build up in the pots and within the soil. To ensure that this happens, give your plants RO water in place of nutrient-rich water.

It is advisable to do flushing at the beginning of every week so that there is no build-up for the rest of the grow cycle. This is only a 24-hour process, and once it is complete, you can get back to your regular feeding schedule.

FLOWER: WEEK 5/6

At this point, all you need is to maintain a clean surrounding and proper feeding. The truth is that these are full-blown weeks when your plants will fatten up more. It is necessary to maintain your pruning and reservoirs until the last week.

During the 5th week, you will notice that the bud sites will start swelling up and the 6th week, there is even further growth of buds. If you see new growth or certain growth dying off, ensure that you prune them off so that your plants are focused more on increasing the harvest.

FLOWER: WEEK 7

This is the week when you don't follow the nutrient feed schedule because all your plants need is freshwater until the time of harvesting. In other words, you are required to do the second and final flush for the remaining two weeks – almost 0 PPM.

The main reason for this is that as your plants start to ripen and reach maturity, they will produce lots of stored energy in the form of sugars within the leaves. You want your plants to cannibalize themselves to lower chemical nutrients in the final crops. This is something that will have an impact on the smell, taste, and overall quality of your plants.

The final flush plays two significant roles;

- Help the plants absorb the remaining nutrients stored in itself
- Flush out anything they would otherwise have taken up through their roots

Note: Any pesticides or toxins taken up by your plants will not be easy to flush out, making them hard to work with.

During this stage, the plant buds will ripen, and the leaves start changing in color. The leaves will turn yellow and begin to die off. The flowers and buds, on the other hand, will get fatter and start swelling.

You don't have to worry much about these events because they are normal. These changes are a sign of nitrogen deficiency, which is okay even though it is known to hinder bud production and growth.

FLOWER: WEEK 8

Bravo! You did it and finally made it to the last week of flowering.

At this point, most of your plants are through with flowering. This means that you must start looking into the harvesting of your plants soon. When we said all plants are different and that they require flowering times, we meant that you must check out your seeds and find out how long they take to flower. Harvest times often vary from 8 weeks to 12 weeks or even in other cases, longer than this.

If you realize that your plants are not ready for harvesting, ensure that you give them all the growing conditions they need to keep growing.

Here, you must keep flushing the remainder nutrients from your plants so that they are ready for their next growth and for you to enjoy the fruits of your labor.

That said, harvesting marijuana is tricky than most people think. It is not like harvesting fruits of veggies, which you may be used to. Therefore, here are some of the things you must know for you to harvest cannabis;

Harvest window

Just like most plants, cannabis has a harvest window. Think about cabbages for a minute – if they stay too long, they might bolt and become inedible. If fruits sit too long on the branches, they over ripen and go bad.

The same applies to marijuana. If they stay too long, they lose their taste and potency. Unlike fruits, sitting on the branches too long makes it hard to determine when to harvest or when not to.

The harvest window for your cannabis plants starts when the buds stop growing white hairs, and approximately 40% of them begin to darken and curl up. When you see this, then you know that you have about a month to chop your plants.

Here are two ways you can figure out when the harvest time has come;

Look at the pestles

When half of your plant's hair curl and darken, it marks the start of the harvest window, and that eventually covers between 60-90% of the plants. The only challenge is that some marijuana strains demonstrate different characteristics at different times. Hence, this technique might not be 100% accurate.

Observe the trichome under the microscope

If the trichome is still clear under a microscope, then know that it is not time to harvest. When they turn cloudy, it means that you can begin harvesting. When they turn amber, then start chopping them down. If you wait too long beyond this, the buds' quality begins to deteriorate or over-ripen, hence not making the quality of your marijuana any better.

What if your yield is not what you desired?

Well, let's face it. There are times when your yield is not ready when you thought it would, but that does not mean that it will not get there. You may want to wait a little longer. It could also indicate that the strain you are working with takes longer to flower. Most strains flower for only eight weeks, but others go to 10-12 weeks.

The best solution here is to find out how long the strain you planted takes to flower. If eight weeks is not enough, then feed your plants a bit longer for them to bloom. Once they do, flush whenever necessary.

There is also a chance that light is leaking around your garden. If you turn the lights off and you can see the light seeping in from the outside of the grow room, give your plants more growth time and darkness to compensate.

Finally, it could also be that they are under heat or light stress. If the environmental conditions are too hot for your plants, there is a chance that the lights are too close to your plants. This will stand in the way of harvesting with plants creating more growth, which is not desired at this point.

11

HARVESTING YOUR MARIJUANA

As we have already discussed, it takes at least 8 hours for indoor cannabis to complete the flowering stage. In the case of outdoor cannabis, it takes even longer for them to be ready for harvest. After waiting for a long time for your marijuana plants to reach maturity, harvesting time comes, and you are happy to eat the fruits of your labor!

Considering the size of your grow space, harvesting your marijuana can be time-consuming. This explains why most marijuana growers choose to turn to mechanical devices for harvesting, hence alleviating labor-associated issues during harvesting.

Just like other crops we are familiar with, marijuana harvesting happens in stages. Although gardens differ from each other and the harvesting techniques vary from one garden to the other, several steps every marijuana grower must follow when it comes to harvesting.

How your marijuana is harvested and processed will greatly impact its quality, longevity, and potency.

If you ask any cannabis horticulturist, they will tell you that commercial operations benefit from streamlining harvest processes.

When efficient processes are in place, the cost of labor is greatly reduced while that of overall returns on investment is increased.

There are three major stages you must follow during the harvest time. These stages are;

- Fan leaf removal
- Trimming and removal of leaves close to the flowers
- Removing flowers from the stem

These three stages only address the physical removal of parts of your marijuana plant. The other crucial stages of harvesting include drying, sorting, and finally curing the cannabis flowers.

STEP 1 FAN LEAF REMOVAL

Once you see that your marijuana plants are ready, the first thing you need to do is get rid of the large fan leaves. These fan leaves are easily identifiable as the stereotypical marijuana leaves. You can pluck these leaves by hand, use a device like a hand-held hedge trimmer or scissors to cut them.

Realize that the large fan leaves you are cutting off do not contain high quantities if cannabinoids compared to the leaves that are much closer to the flowers or the flowers themselves. Because of that, most advanced growers choose to dispose of them. Once these fan leaves are removed, you have two choices;

- Trim the remaining leaf material while your marijuana plants are still wet – otherwise referred to as wet trimming.
- Start the drying process and get rid of the remaining leaf materials, either using your hands or an automated trimmer once the plants are dry.

STEP 2 DRYING

You must note that drying the cannabis plants can be achieved by either wet trimming or immediately the large fan leaves are removed – if you opt for the dry trim method.

You must take your marijuana plants and hang them upside down to dry.

You can also cut them into smaller, more manageable pieces or dry them as an entire plant. The ideal drying conditions for your cannabis are temperatures of between 65- and 75-degrees Fahrenheit. The required drying humidity levels must range between 45 and 55%.

It is advisable to do your drying in total darkness. This is mainly because the UV light from the sun or artificial lights risk damaging some of the high sorts after cannabinoids or terpenes in the flowers.

Generally, the drying process should take at least 7-10 days for your marijuana plant to dry completely. You will know when the drying process is complete because you can easily bend the stem of a dried plant as well as the stem snaps.

STEP 3 DESTEMMING

If you choose to wet trim your plants as a way of drying them, it is recommended that you destem the flowers and store them in appropriate holding bags for curing.

Alternatively, if you choose a dry trim and wish to use an automated trimmer, you must start the destemming process once the plants are completely dry. You can use a sharp pair of scissors to cut off the base of the flowers to remove them from the central stalk.

Even though most marijuana growers destem by hand or using scissors, there are several automated devices you can use to separate the flowers from the stem. Automation is something that not only makes the destemming process easy but also saves time if you have many plants – especially when you are running a commercial cannabis operation.

STEP 4 SORTING

This is one of the most important steps in maximizing the efficiency of your harvest process. When you separate the flowers into various sizes, you are in a better position to process your marijuana flowers more efficiently and effectively.

For instance, if you process the same-sized flower materials in an automatic trim machine, the trimming process is not only effective but also time saving and labor-intensive. When you automate the sorting process, this has a great impact on the harvest process, especially if you run a large-scale cannabis operation.

Once you have your cannabis flowers fully sorted, you can process them further in a trim machine, among other processing machines, based on size. You can also sort them once the trimming process is complete. Sorting your trimmed cannabis flowers based on size can make them more marketable.

STEP 5 TRIMMING

Once you are done dry trimming, a process that is often tedious and slow, and sorting, you can further trim your cannabis plants. The trimming process must be done using the right machinery to get that hand-trimmed look while still ensuring that you maintain its quality and save time.

During the drying process, you can stick the leaves against the flowers and hang them to dry, thanks to gravity's force. The main purpose of doing a dry trim, in this case, is to get rid of the leaf material that surrounds the flowers as much as you can. This will, in turn, expose the flowers, which are the most potent parts of your marijuana plant.

You will need multiple workers to complete the work in the shortest time when you do dry trimming by hand. The only problem with this is that hiring people is very expensive. In most instances, you will need to micromanage your workers and increase the security measures around your grow space.

This explains why most serious and advanced growers choose to use automated machines to do the trimming. Once the flowers are completely dried and destemmed, you can place them in an automated trim machine for a final manicure before they are taken for curing.

The trimming will have to take place during the drying process if you opt for a wet trim. Most growers often choose a wet trim because it is easy to access the leaves and hastens the process. For small grow operations – most especially beginners – it is advisable that the trimming is done by hand, and a wet trim is the most efficient way to go.

However, in the case of large cannabis operations where most growers choose to use automated devices, trimming your materials once the marijuana flowers are completely dried is the most efficient way to go.

STEP 6 CURING

This is the grand finale of the harvesting process. It must be done once the trimming process is complete.

During the curing process, you must note that the flowers continue drying slowly. This is very important in ensuring that the flavors are enriched. The containers you use for the curing process must be stored in a cool and dark place where you can examine them every day.

For the first two weeks of curing, ensure that the storage containers are burped at least once or twice a day. This goes a long way in allowing some of the built-up humidity out and fresh air in. After these first two weeks, you can open the containers less frequently – at least once or twice a week.

After a couple of months, the curing process should be complete. Your marijuana flowers should be at the peak of their flavors. If you do the curing process properly, you stand to prolong the shelf life of your marijuana flowers – in terms of flavors, potency, and odors.

Just like the harvest process of other crops, that of marijuana has no one right way to do it. However, automation is quickly becoming commonplace among cannabis growers, and that requires them to follow a specific method to maximize both efficiency and effectiveness.

If you run a commercial cannabis operation, you must ensure that you invest in tools required for trimming, sorting, and destemming. These tools will help you remain in an ever-changing and highly competitive market. These tools will go a long way in reducing labor costs while ensuring that your marijuana flowers are processed fast and efficiently to preserve its flavors, smells, and potency.

OUTDOOR CULTIVATION OF CANNABIS

Cannabis has thrived in the outdoors for hundreds of years. As an aspiring grower, you should be able to try outdoor cultivation at least once. Perhaps, the main factors that can stop you from doing so include the law, the lack of outdoor space, and the thought of kids, pets, or someone else messing up your marijuana plants. If you are allowed and have the space to do so, then try it. Regarding kids, pets, or other persons who might mess up your home plantation, you can set up a fence to protect your plants from intrusion.

There are many benefits to outdoor marijuana cultivation. With this method, you do not need to buy pots unless you are going to do it on your veranda or roof deck. You can take advantage of sunlight, rainwater, and carbon dioxide as well. This also allows you to apply organic farming methods that are organic. All of these make outdoor cultivation less expensive than indoor cultivation. Cannabis plants are hardy thanks to their growth in the wild for years, so the preparation of your planting site should not be that hard. Another good thing about this is that you can yield more because you can use plants with better foliage. With such, the leaves can undergo photosynthesis that will provide the plant with more energy to produce the flowers later on. Remember that it is called a weed for a reason. It can grow nearly in the most random of places and sometimes, in the most random of times. The derivatives from outdoor marijuana plants are also known to have better taste and aroma.

To reap the benefits of outdoor marijuana cultivation, you have to spend much time on garden preparation. Getting all your gears ready makes the latter steps of cultivation easier and quicker.

Garden Preparation

It is best to start your garden preparation during early springtime. Make it a part of your annual spring cleaning. Instead of just de-cluttering your home, you should also get rid of the garden waste that the previous season left by in your yard once you are done with a general cleanup of your yard. It is time to choose a spot for your mini marijuana plantation.

Location

You should pick a location where your marijuana plants will receive sunlight the most. Therefore, areas near or under the trees or the awnings of your home are not ideal. Additionally, the location should be away from areas where there is standing water. The plants will be under high stress if you do so. Aside from that, standing water may attract pests. You should also consider the spacing between your plants (3 to 5 feet away from each other). This allows your plants to grow freely and to allow you to move between them with so much ease. You should plan and set up the drainage for your garden when you are done picking the right location. If you are setting up your garden in a veranda or roof deck, make sure your plants will be elevated. The flooring may be too warm, especially if tiled that it may put the roots of your marijuana plants in high stress. You can elevate your plants by setting a platform using wood since the material is a good insulator of heat. You can simply create a rectangular box and drill holes where you will place the pots. Coat your wooden platform with a water-resistant finish. Make sure there are trays or saucers below the pots. These are meant to catch run-off water from the potted plants.

Soil

The first thing you need to do is to get rid of grasses or weeds on your planting location. The sight of these organisms might mean trouble, but their presence indicates that the site is good for marijuana plants. If you have other valued plants in it, transfer it somewhere else. Use a rake to remove debris in the area further. You do not want the possibility of a random piece of broken glass blocking or hurting the root of your upcoming marijuana plants. Getting your soil ready requires checking its pH level. You can buy a soil testing kit from most gardening stores to know the soil's pH level. There is no such thing as perfect soil for marijuana cultivation, but the ideal pH level of your soil should fall within 5.8 to 6.5.

If your soil's pH level is not within the said range, you have to improve it by adding compost and other organic fertilizers such as bone meal, blood meal, worm castings, aged manure, and bat guano.

You may add some biodegradable mulch as well. Chemical fertilizers are more readily available, but they can hurt your soil in the long run, preventing you from planting regularly. Once your soil gets polluted, you have to let it rest for a while and treat it with organic soil amendments.

The soil type in your yard matters as well. The soil testing kit you are going to buy is likely to have a tool that can help you know whether your soil is clay, sand, or loam. You can simply rely on your observation, too. Clay tends to stick together while sand is too loose. Loamy soil is the most ideal because it may stick together, but it drains well, highly preferred by marijuana plants. Loam contains silt, sand, clay, and organic matter.

Find out what kind of soil you have, grab a fistful of soil, and squeeze it. If it tends to form a ball, it is probably clay, and you might need to boost the amount of silt, sand, and organic matter in your soil. If it tends to crumble, it is probably sand, and you might have to add clay, silt, and organic matter to balance it.

When you are done creating it, pour water in your soil. If it drains well yet remains moist, you have achieved the type of soil that is conducive to your marijuana cultivation.

Water Supply

Marijuana plants require lots of water to thrive. You will not have much problem if you live in a place where it rains a lot. If it rarely rains in your place even in springtime, you should buy an extensive hose or place a water faucet nearby. It pays to have a stream or other bodies of water near your place as well. You can get water from the bodies of water for free, but it takes a lot of time and effort.

Protection

Your outdoor marijuana plants have three main enemies: wind, animals, and humans. There is nothing much you can do to control the wind, but if there is a hilly side in your place, you may use such as a natural shield against the wind. If there are no hills, you have no other choice but to set up a fence. This does not only protect your plants against the wind but possibly against large animals and humans as well. That is not enough, though. You need to surround your mini marijuana plantation with thorny bushes to prevent small animals like rabbits from messing up your garden. You may also plant other taller plants, such as maize. Elderberry and bamboo are both good shields for marijuana plants as well.

Once everything is ready, you can start your hunt for the best strains for outdoor marijuana cultivation. While waiting for your seeds, decide the germination methods you have to employ. Pick at least two. For outdoor cultivation, you might want to germinate some of your seeds directly on the grounds. If you are opting for starter cubes, purchase them before you buy seeds. After germinating some seeds indoors, you can transfer them to pots for a while. Let them grow indoors first while the outdoor seeds remain. Keep their soil moist but not too wet or too soaking. For the indoor seedlings, give them 24 hours of light. Transfer them outdoors after 3 to 4 weeks.

Plant Care

After transplanting the seedlings, you are bound to face the most tiring part of marijuana cultivation. This requires you to be observant of how you handle your plants and how they respond to the care you provide.

Vegetative Phase

After the seedling phase, your plants will enter the so-called vegetative phase, usually in the second month after germination. In this phase, the plants will do nothing but grow more leaves and stems. They are going to need lots of water, nutrients, and sunlight.

You should water your plants every other day if it does not rain much in your place during this stage. If it rains a lot in one week, you might not need to water at all. When it comes to nutrients, you should provide nitrogen, phosphorus, and potassium (NPK). The ratio between the three macronutrients should be 10-5-7. Add some micronutrients such as zinc, molybdenum, magnesium, and iron as well. You can buy all of these from your preferred gardening stores.

As for the sunlight, you cannot do much about it. However, if there are trees in your yard that tends to over your marijuana plants, you should trim the branches of the said trees.

Pre-flowering Phase

The phase between the vegetative and flowering stages is also known as the stretch. This one only takes 10 to 14 days, though. (The vegetative and flowering phases take a month or more.) In this stage, you should gradually increase the water supply and nutrients you give to your marijuana plants. As to the nutrients, you should adjust the ratio of NPK to 5-10-7 or 5-50-17.

In this phase, you have to do the elimination of your male marijuana plants. Do not wait until the 14th day before you proceed with this task. Male marijuana plants tend to mature faster than their female counterparts do, so you should act as soon as possible. Remember to look at the appearance of the buds. Male buds tend to resemble small balls while female buds have hairs.

Flowering Phase

This stage may take 6 to 22 weeks. This is the stage where you can finally see the possible quality and quantity of your harvest. If you are using chemical fertilizers, you have to lessen the supply during the flowering stage to prevent the flowers from tasting and smelling like chemicals.

Stop supplying nutrients altogether in the last two weeks. In this phase, the plant will stop growing, but it will focus more on producing flowers.

STATES THAT RECENTLY LEGALIZED CANNABIS

U *tah*

Medicinal marijuana will be on the November 2018 voting form in Utah, after rivals of authorization dropped their claim in June. Even though the state has an enormous populace of Mormons, who restrict the utilization of liquor or medications, 75 percent of voters state they will cast a ballot for the activity.

Update: Utah voters passed Proposition 1 in the November 2018 political race, favoring restorative marijuana. However, the state will sanction an elective law. Partners on the two sides of the issue arrived at this trade-off in October to guarantee a type of medicinal marijuana arrangement, paying little respect to the vote.

The state's variant will change a portion of the subtleties permitted in the voting form measure, including the evacuation of the home development arrangement and a decrease in dispensaries and qualifying ailments.

Nevada

Alongside California and two different states, Nevada cast a ballot to legitimize recreational cannabis in 2016, and the subsequent measures produced results the next year. Keeping pace with past markets, the underlying recreational permit application was open just to therapeutic marijuana dispensaries on favorable terms. Projections for open recreational market applications are when October 2018 and as late as July 2019. With dazzling early deals and an inspirational viewpoint, this might be another grower's most logical option.

Maine

Maine got one of the primary states on the east coast to sanction marijuana. Question 1 showed up on the 2016 voting form and passed just barely with 50.26% of the vote. The resistance requested a describe, however, rejected it because of cost and no significant differences in casting a ballot appropriation.

Preceding statewide authorization, a few urban communities in Maine (counting crowded Portland, South Portland, and Lewiston) have just sanctioned belonging and utilization of cannabis by grown-ups inside city limits.

The activity licenses clients 21 and over to have up to 2.5 ounces of marijuana and six develop plants. It's additionally the primary state to permit "social clubs" for cannabis to enable clients to expand retail recreational items on-premises.

Confinements apply. Guests to cannabis social clubs must utilize items there and not ship them off the property. In like manner, retail locations can't enable benefactors to open and devour their buys inside the store. Cannabis clients would likewise be not able to use off-site cannabis at social clubs. Offices can open when February 2018.

Vermont

Vermont is the most up to date expansion to the growing rundown of states that have authorized recreational cannabis. Starting on July 1, 2018, grown-ups beyond 21 years old have up to one ounce of cannabis, and grow two develop and four youthful plants in their home. The plants must be screened from general visibility, and just those more than 21 can approach. Inhabitants who are leasing need to get consent from their landowner to grow at home, in any case, proprietors are not required to concede authorization if they boycott growing tasks on their property, the occupant must go along.

Michigan

Michigan's association with cannabis has been combative since therapeutic marijuana laws were passed in 2008, yet the two activities to authorize cannabis this year each show guarantee. Because the state governing body continually reconsiders guidelines around medicinal marijuana, administrators are compelled to remain in business at the ever-present danger of arraignment.

While restorative marijuana is still accessible for occupants, an activity to sanction recreational utilize was not able to jump on the 2016 polling form.

Update: Proponents, as of late, gathered enough marks to get authorization of recreational cannabis on the November 2018 polling form. As per late surveys, 61 percent of voters will cast a ballot yes on this measure.

Update: In November 2018, Michigan turned into the tenth state in the U.S. to sanction recreational cannabis. Recommendation 1 earned 55.9 percent of the vote, authorizing the ownership and development of cannabis by grown-ups 21 years and over. The principal retail businesses will probably be open by 2020.

Missouri

Missouri is a longshot for those considering a passage to a lawful cannabis market. The state is without a therapeutic marijuana program or cannabis advocates in the state or official governing body, making sanctioning an impressive longshot for cheerful Missourians. While the state's endeavors to authorize CBD cannabis removes for individuals experiencing epilepsy and seizures, it is anything but a patient-accommodating condition. Just two non-benefit associations are allowed to create and convey cannabis oil in Missouri. This means a system of competent and experienced growers isn't probably going to develop very soon.

New Approach Missouri, the crusade to sanction medicinal marijuana, accumulated enough marks to get activity on the November 2018 polling form. It is anything but a slam dunk yet, however, as they are anticipating affirmation that it will be up for a vote this year.

Update: In November 2018, voters in Missouri passed Amendment 2, the state-protected revision sanctioning therapeutic cannabis. The new law permits patients who qualify and get doctor endorsement to grow up to six marijuana plants, purchase 4 ounces of dried marijuana, and have a 60-day supply of dried marijuana. Specialists can endorse medicinal marijuana for any condition they feel justifies this treatment. Income from deals duty will go to veterans' administrations.

On June 4, 2019, Missouri's Department of Health and Senior Services will make applications for patient cards and businesses accessible; it will start tolerating them beginning July 4, 2019.

Missouri authorities have not gone to an accord on whether therapeutic marijuana clients will be denied state occupations or welfare benefits.

Missouri voters didn't endorse the other two cannabis activities on the November 2018 voting form — Amendment 2 and Proposition C — which were likewise medicinal marijuana activities yet with marginally different insights about belonging sums and expense revenue distribution.

Oklahoma

Oklahoma voters passed State Question 788 in June 2018, legitimizing medicinal marijuana. The unavoidable trends are blowing through this red state, as they are one of only a handful, not many that enable specialists to prescribe cannabis for any ailment regarded fitting. Other states' therapeutic marijuana laws just permit its proposal for specific maladies.

A few changes to this law might be sanctioned, notwithstanding, as Governor Fallin stresses that this law has, generally, legitimized recreational use. The truth will surface, eventually, how this specific case turns out.

Canada

Our neighbor toward the north has authorized the clearance of certain types of recreational cannabis. Beginning on October 17, 2018, it will be legitimate for those beyond 18 years old to purchase crisp or dried cannabis, cannabis oil, and seeds or starts for development. Starting now, edibles are not lawful. However, that is gotten ready for some other time. The trading and bringing in of cannabis is unlawful, except for restorative and scientific use, which will require a license.

The law enables individuals to grow up to four plants on their property, yet plans are set up to permit bigger growing tasks, with limits. "Miniaturized scale" growers with crops no bigger than 200 square meters, or around 2,150 square feet, might be authorized. Breaking points on ownership, growing, singular areas can set age and lawful use territories.

Canada drafted rules for the bundling of cannabis even under the steady gaze of the law passed. Lawful cannabis items in Canada must have plain bundles with just well-being alerts, and one brand stamping permitted.

STATES CONSIDERING LEGAL CANNABIS

Arizona

Full sanctioning of cannabis endured a shot in Arizona. Suggestion 205 would have permitted individuals 21 and over to utilize marijuana recreationally. The measure additionally allowed clients to grow up to 6 plants. Even though the recommendation would apply 80% of duty income from deals to class regions and sanction schools inside Arizona, it fizzled. The voting form had 51.32% democratic no on the recommendation.

While it stays illicit for Arizona occupants to utilize recreational marijuana, earlier recommendations 200 and 203 are still as a result. The measures enable individuals with specific conditions to have marijuana for therapeutic use.

Connecticut

The table seems set for legitimization in Connecticut, with a fruitful medicinal marijuana program propelled in 2012 and an uplifting standpoint at a few surveys. Besides, law authorization in Connecticut is now getting ready for cannabis sanctioning and preparing officials to all the more likely identify and test for THC levels in drivers.

Rhode Island

Rhode Island bested Colorado, Washington, and each other state in the association for the most elevated level of cannabis clients saying they've expended cannabis inside the most recent month – for a long time running.

That doesn't mean authorization is a certain wagered for the small Northeastern state. Enactment pushed in 2015 neglected to flourish, and keeping in mind that surveying information looks encouraging, 2016 may not be the year the Ocean State completely sanctions.

States That Have Not Legalized Cannabis

Delaware

There's just a solitary therapeutic marijuana dispensary inactivity in Delaware, and only 700 patients enrolled under current necessity, leaving possibilities for recreational sanctioning desolate, best case scenario. While Governor Jack Markell did to be sure to sign a decriminalization bill late 2015, statewide authorization presently can't seem to occur.

Maryland

Maryland is attempting to actualize a successful therapeutic marijuana market. However, if state enactment presented a year ago finds a ground well of help among officials, a recreational market in Maryland may need to pause. Over 50 percent of occupants bolster statewide legitimization, yet almost certainly, the state will bolster a recreational market before its therapeutic marijuana business gets this show on the road.

New York

The State of New York is setting up a significant push toward executing a medicinal marijuana program. However, the weight applied to the only five authorized makers to grow and sell enough items by January could incite a deferral in accomplishing full legitimization statewide.

In June, New York moved to seal the records of low-level medication feelings to improve the conditions of those influenced by over 40 years of "hyper-criminalization." While this flag softens toward general demeanors toward cannabis, the way to recreational cannabis remains soundly through a fruitful sending of a medicinal marijuana program.

South Dakota

The "Coyote State" accumulated more than the necessary number of marks to jump on the voting form, however, Secretary of State Shantel Krebs dismissed the petitions because not every one of the marks was legitimate.

South Dakota is the main state to make it illicit to test positive for cannabinoids regardless of whether the medication was expended in a state where it is legitimate. This "inside belonging" law conveys a stiff punishment of a year in prison and a $2,000 fine for sure.

ONE LAST WORD

Beginners almost always make mistakes. However, every step you take is a learning curve, and growing marijuana at home is no different. If you have been growing weed for at least a few years, you are better at it than individuals who are just starting.

In growing marijuana, know some of the mistakes that more experienced marijuana cultivators had committed when they first began. The following may help you avoid problems in the course of your hobby. Do not talk to anyone. Talking about growing your marijuana is a no-no. Keep your hobby to yourself.

Be prepared. When you grow marijuana, you may face uncertainties that can overwhelm you. You should consider the plants 'needs like nutrients, water, carbon dioxide, and light. You should also be prepared for other matters like lack of nutrient quality, bug infestations, and insufficient carbon dioxide amounts. Have a contingency plan in case your plants manifest negative signs.

Window growth is not enough. Sunlight is the perfect light source for any plant. However, growing your plants indoors and using the window as your only source of light doesn't cut it. Marijuana plants need as much light, and even sunlight is not enough. If you're growing them indoors, buy lights.

Even if your marijuana plants grow, they won't thrive the way you intend them to. Many fertilizers have an NPK ratio displayed conveniently on the packaging. NPK describes the combination of N (nitrogen), P (phosphorus), and K (potassium) as they related to each other.

For each period of growth, excluding the flowering period, you may want to utilize a fertilizer with a higher nitrogen concentration than anything else. When your plants are in the flowering stage, you should use a fertilizer with more phosphorus.

Growing cannabis in a nursery is comparable here and there to growing different yields, for example, ornamentals and vegetables. Cannabis, like most plants, requires the correct plant supplements, the right measure of water, and the fitting amount of light to stay sound. A controlled domain, such as a nursery, enables growers to meet these necessities by giving the capacity to control encouraging, light levels (daylight or artificial), mugginess, temperature, and so on.

Despite the similitudes in meeting essential plant needs to grow a quality harvest, there are a few key factors a grower ought to consider when hoping to grow cannabis, particularly when contrasted with customary vegetable yields. First off, cannabis must be grown to pass each state's trying qualifications to be endorsed for circulation and deal.

Perhaps the greatest difference I've found in the business between growing cannabis or different yields depends on the edge or gainfulness that the cannabis crop at present directions. From ecological controllers to lighting, light hardship, and coating choices, I see more cash being spent on framework than I have ever found in a practically identical vegetable activity.

Cooling is the ideal model. Customarily, most growers could never utilize cooling in a nursery. Numerous vegetable nurseries will utilize cooling somehow, yet it is ordinarily evaporative cooling. Why would that be? Other than nurseries being generally wasteful structures, most growers essentially can't justify the related expenses in a vegetable and elaborate activity. In the cannabis market, where item costs and edges are a lot higher, growers can justify a device like cooling.

No grower at any point stated, "I wish I had less command over this condition." Similar to the cooling idea, there are numerous instances of cannabis offices that are littler than ¼ of a section of land, yet they have natural control PCs that are north of six figures. Cannabis plants flourish in ideal conditions, and a controller assists take with excursion the mystery while limiting space for mistake. Cloud-observing frameworks, for instance, make it simple for growers to remotely screen dampness, temperature, CO_2, and supplement levels, and the sky is the limit. Each grower who uses some type of controlled condition agribusiness can profit by a natural controller, regardless of whether it's on a fundamental level of clocks and indoor regulators, or as convoluted and controlled as can be envisioned.

Cannabis plants are substantial feeders, much like tomatoes, and increment their admission when in the blooming state. Consequently, a supplement infusion framework that can nourish different zones is effective in eliminating work costs and guaranteeing exactness in the arrangement being sustained to the plants.

Typical practice with cannabis plants is to flush them toward the end of a growth cycle by bolstering the plant's pH-adjusted water of 5.8 to 6.2 for a few days, which flushes out all the compost from its life cycle. This guarantees the item is free of remaining salts, which is a prerequisite in most state testing rules.

If you grow any kind of plant in a nursery, you have most likely encountered a period in which you wished you had all the more light. A controlled-situation structure regularly has supplemental lighting to compensate for lower light levels throughout the winter months or on shady, cloudy days.

Numerous cannabis growers need to light for the full sun because there might be seasons of the year where they should have their light-hardship framework shut; however, they will at present need a 12-hour light cycle. This often occurs because of a light contamination statute. Numerous urban communities and regions have exacting zoning rules or guidelines concerning light contamination. Cannabis structures can be dependent upon extra prerequisites (smell control, road permeability, security, etc.) that can be incredibly expensive if not represented in the underlying undertaking stages.

Nuisance and infection control are zones often neglected, in cannabis offices as well as in vegetable activities, too. Nuisance and illness, the executives are considerably progressively basic with cannabis plants because of the stringent testing laws managing the market. A larger part of nursery vermin comes in through unscreened vents, but regardless I see numerous offices with no sort of creepy-crawly screening or aversion.

It's essential to have an arrangement set up to avert significant episodes as opposed to attempting to speed and battle a previously existing issue. This can be accomplished by presenting helpful bugs, or by executing a mist/showering framework at a convenient time.

Likewise, with all farming, there are no obvious responses for how to grow or how to make progress in the cannabis market. There are just answers of differing accuracy that will work better or more awful for every grower dependent on their circumstance and condition. The greatest takeaway is that growing cannabis, similar to every other plant, requires careful consideration and arranging. My best guidance is to inquire about your hardware accomplices, visit comparative activities, and gain from others in the business who can help bolster you.

Be active. Growing marijuana requires much of your time. You need to care for them as you would your child. Marijuana plants have short lifespans, from fertilization to harvest, and you just can't plant them and leave them alone. Make sure your plants get adequate ventilation, CO2, and light. Feed them, prune them, trim them, pamper them, and water them.

Not all soils are equal. A lot of newbie marijuana growers may think that any outdoor soil has enough nutrients for their plants. That soil, unfortunately, may only be 'glorified dirt. 'That soil may be too alkaline or too acidic and won't help to properly germinate your seeds. When you grow marijuana outdoors, infuse your soil with potting mix or fertilizer. Also, have a pH balance test to make sure the soil's pH is near 7.0.

Don't over-prune. Pruning a plant does encourage growth, and you may have heard that more pruning means more growth. It may be true, but you don't have to prune down a marijuana plant in its entirety. You may only weaken it or even kill it if you prune your plant too much.

Don't root-bound the plants. You may not know that marijuana roots grow fast. When the plants are placed in a container, the roots usually line the container's walls and go down to the bottom. If your container is too small, your plants can get root-bound, and they can die. Carefully transfer the plants to bigger containers after they have manifested accelerated growth.

Don't panic. The problems that occur when growing marijuana plants are from mistakes that can be avoided or reversed. If the plants begin to wilt and some leaves turn yellow, for example, it could be because of a missing nutrient. Some leaves will just die off either because of natural processes or lack of light. Generally, it does not indicate a greater problem.

Educate yourself. You will make fewer mistakes if you are well informed. Other people make the most mistakes before you start to grow it, so know their mistakes and learn from them.

If you don't have a daily maintenance plan for every problem, the truth is that you might get frustrated when one leads to the other. If unaddressed, you risk spiraling to another, and you end up wasting a whole grow. At least spend some time every day – 10 to 15 minutes – performing simple checks in your grow space to ensure that everything is working as required. This way, you will be able to keep everything flowing smoothly and end up with a high harvest grow and get ahead of all the issues you run into along the way.

So, what are you still waiting for?

It is time to get those pretty hands dirty, and after a couple of months, you will be smiling all the way to the bank!

Best Wishes!

PSILOCYBIN MUSHROOMS

THE ULTIMATE STEP-BY-STEP GUIDE TO CULTIVATION AND SAFE USE OF PSYCHEDELIC MUSHROOMS - LEARN HOW TO GROW MAGIC MUSHROOMS, ENJOY THEIR BENEFITS, AND MANAGE THEIR SIDE-EFFECTS

INTRODUCTION

Welcome to the world of psychedelics! Here we are.

You have probably heard of psilocybin mushrooms. If not, then, worry not. This book is about you and those who wish to learn more. Psychedelics? Psilocybin? Do not get scared by these two big terms. Behind them rests simple feelings. Psychedelics are those substances that, when you consume them, they take you into another world of imaginations. Psilocybin is just one of those psychedelic substances commonly found in mushrooms. Psilocybin is the marriage bond between mushrooms and psychedelics.

Not all mushrooms are psychedelic. Only a few species exist that nature chose to hide in them this potent magic. A potency that when consumed, brings new realities to the perception of the nature of things and the nature of beings. If you have never witnessed your mind concocting a new magnificent reality right before your sight, this experience can be a miracle. Yet, this is not new. The gods of our ancestors made them experience this long before we were born. It is our turn to pass over this magic to our future generations. This book is just about that – to let you experience this magical reality, and from that experience, you can narrate your experience to them as a first-hand witness.

Behind this new phenomenal reality, your mental reformation takes place - Stress disappears. Anxiety dies. Calmness settles. Your brain-power gets re-energized. Thus, it is not just the sensations that matter. No. Those are merely beautiful symptoms of some great mental transformations taking place behind the curtain of your conscious mind. It is a renewal. It is a rebirth - of the entire mind.

There are many psychedelics, but I have decided to bring psilocybin. Why psilocybin? There is a reason why I am recommending this potion. The nature of psilocybin makes it compelling. It has a host of therapeutic benefits to your health that you cannot afford to miss. Later in this book, I will unveil to you plenty of reasons as to why psilocybin is ideal for you.

WHY NOT OTHER PSYCHEDELICS?

Yes, there is LSD. LSD is probably the most potent of all psychedelics. It is much more potent than the mushroom's psilocybin. However, it is synthetic – with not-so-pleasant side effects. It is not natural. Yet, its synthesis is such complex that it can only be done in the labs by qualified experts. What about psilocybin mushrooms? Well, our ancestors knew how to use them – as illiterate as they were. They did not need a lab. They did not need a technical degree. Nothing but the sheer taste of their tongue buds.

So, you don't need to be an expert to get the benefits of psilocybin found in the mushrooms. All you need is the knowledge of what these types of mushrooms are, where to find them, how to grow them right in your home, and how to consume them. It would be such complex to set an LSD lab in your home, and extremely risky.

WHY NOT ANY OTHER KIND OF MUSHROOMS?

Nature knows how to be fair. There are mushrooms for life (food and healing); there are mushrooms for heaven (leisure and relaxation), and there are mushrooms for 'death' (toxic or poisonous). Yet, even within each category, some species are more potent in their respective category than others.

Why Psilocybin mushrooms? Psilocybin mushrooms are the mushrooms for heaven. They are the gods' secret potent. They are the ones endowed with the power to drive you to 'high' heavens. They are the only ones with the potency of this naturally-occurring psychedelic substance – psilocybin.

ARE PSILOCYBIN MUSHROOMS LEGAL?

Laws are not static, but dynamic. Throughout history, there are many things which had been criminalized only to be legalized later due to their immense benefits to society. One such case is marijuana. Marijuana was once criminalized across the world. However, due to the overwhelming scientific discoveries of its immense medical benefits, many countries have now decriminalized its use for medicinal purposes. The same is the case with psilocybin mushrooms. The immense scientific evidence of the mental health benefits of psilocybin mushrooms has meant that many jurisdictions are now reversing the criminalization laws.

Not all countries move at the same pace of development. There will always be laggards. Thus, it is important to find out whether your country allows you to grow or consume psilocybin mushrooms or not before you take up the trip to this psychedelic world.

Can I have my own psilocybin mushrooms garden?

Yes, you can grow psilocybin mushrooms – right in your home. You do not need acreages of land. Just some little space in your spare room is enough. You can even use some space in your garage, balcony, or even verandah! All you need to ensure is that you create the right conditions for the mushrooms to grow, flourish, and pump in the psilocybin.

With a simple knowledge of how to grow container plants, you can easily grow your own psilocybin mushrooms and get that psychedelic potency right within your reach. You can experience the world of your ancestors and that of your future descendants - right in the present – psilocybin is the magic! No lab required. No complex expertise needed—only the magic mushrooms.

I am going to show you how to select the right materials and the right tools, how to prepare the right substrate, how to set the right temperature and light conditions. And, ultimately, how to tend to your budding mushrooms up to maturity.

How do I harvest, treat, and store my psilocybin mushrooms?

Apart from the growing environment, the potency of psilocybin depends heavily on how the mushroom is treated and stored after harvest. Furthermore, the extra benefits such as Vitamin D and other essential minerals are significantly enhanced through proper treatment and storage.

In this book, I will show you how to harvest, treat, and store your magic mushrooms so that you get the most optimal psychedelic effect, plus other health benefits.

What is the best way for me to consume my psychedelic mushrooms?

Just like other foods, having the best ingredients does not necessarily guarantee you a delicious meal. Bad cooks turning great ingredients into a horrible meal is almost a proverb. It takes a mastery of culinary arts to achieve a great meal. This is the reason why I have indulged myself in showing you how to consume your delicious psilocybin mushrooms. You will learn different methods of consuming your beloved mushrooms, how to derive the consumable extracts, and the different recipes you need to make you savor the magical taste while keeping monotony at bay.

This book is a delicacy in its regard. Keep sampling more. Tons of sumptuous knowledge beckons you to devour.

Can I have a life-long transforming experience with these magic mushrooms?

Sure! The magic part of psychedelic mushrooms is that you create and sustain a life-long experience out of consuming them. What you need is to have a daily micro-dose of psilocybin. This micro-dose is powerful enough to boost your mental acuity yet, light enough not to export you into another world permanently.

With the various methods of consumption and several recipes provided in this book, you can enjoy an endless magical lifestyle.

SO, WHAT NEXT?

Dive deep into this world of psychedelics. Get started with the first Part, and more will keep flowing as you enjoy this highly sensual psychedelic immersion. Keep reading…

I

WHY PSILOCYBIN MUSHROOMS?

A forest of magic mushrooms. Image source: pxfuel.com

OVERVIEW

Those who are yet to experience the magic potency of psilocybin mushrooms are left wondering, "why psilocybin mushrooms?'

This is the big question that I am going to answer in this Part. While the answer could be as simple as having a bite of this magic mushroom, it is better to know in advance what to expect.

I am going to explain to you what makes this mushroom gain its magic powers, the kind of benefits it bestows to your health, and why it is ideal for you.

TOPICS COVERED

- The nature of psilocybin mushrooms
- Therapeutic benefits of psilocybin
- Why magic mushrooms are ideal for you

1

THE NATURE OF PSILOCYBIN MUSHROOMS

The best way to know, understand, and appreciate psilocybin mushrooms is to master the details about their nature. First of all, you need to know their physical characteristics. This will help you distinguish them from other species. Secondly, you need to know their chemical composition, which is their common bond (psilocybin). Thirdly, you need to understand the chemical composition and pharmacological characteristics of psilocybin – the potent compound responsible for the magical effect. Lastly, you need to understand how psilocybin works to achieve this magical effect.

PHYSICAL CHARACTERISTICS OF PSILOCYBIN MUSHROOMS

With almost 200 species of psilocybin mushrooms, it is hard to come to common physical characteristics. However, as a rule of thumb, we can outline some common features, even though they might not apply to all the psilocybes.

IDENTIFYING THE MAGIC MUSHROOMS

With almost 200 species of psychedelic mushrooms out of thousands of mushroom species, it is a daunting task to distinguish between psychedelic and non-psychedelic mushrooms.

Nonetheless, two fundamental attributes (according to Stametsian Rule) can help us separate the magic from the non-magic. Psychedelic mushrooms have:

- Bruise blue flesh
- Gilled, with a purple-brown or black spore print

Apart from these general attributes, each species of psilocybe has a unique identity. With almost 200 species of psilocybes, we cannot afford to give specific identities of each in this book. Nonetheless, we have described the general attributes to look out for when choosing your preferred species of psilocybin mushroom for planting.

PARTS OF THE MAGIC MUSHROOMS

Apart from features described under the Stametsian Rule, magic mushrooms are largely similar to other types of mushrooms in terms of their main parts.

The following diagram depicts the major parts of a psychedelic mushroom:

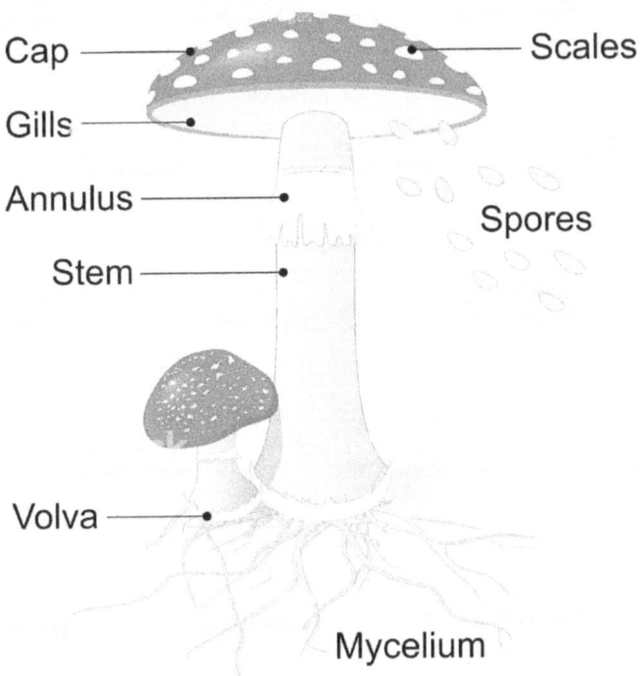

Parts of a magic mushroom. Image source: Istockphoto.com

CHEMICAL COMPOSITION OF PSILOCYBIN

Psilocybin is a tryptamine alkaloid extracted from various types of fungi. When ingested, psilocybin is converted into pharmacologically active form psilocin. While psilocin also exists in psychedelic mushrooms, it is in trace quantities. Thus, the bulk of the psychedelic effect is derived from the converted psilocin rather than from the naturally occurring psilocin.

PHARMACOLOGICAL CHARACTERISTICS OF PSILOCYBIN

Psilocybin is a psychotropic drug, which means that it is a drug that has a psychedelic effect. It is regarded as a psychedelic prodrug. A prodrug is a chemical compound that is pharmacologically inactive. However, after getting consumed, it becomes activated through the body's metabolism.

As a Type 1B prodrug, Psilocybin is activated intracellularly, that is, within the cell membrane. Typical cells affected by psilocybin include the liver cells, brain cells, mucosal GI cell, lung, among others.

The pharmacological evolution of psilocybin mushrooms

Psilocybin mushrooms evolved to adapt to its harsh conditions. Initially, this magic mushroom was just like other mushrooms – without psilocybin. However, due to the need to survive against ants and such other predators, the mushroom started to develop psilocybin chemicals as a defense mechanism.

The psilocybin chemical acted as a way of making the ants easily get satiated and thus eat less of the mushrooms. This ensures more mushrooms survive to maturity.

WHAT PSILOCYBIN MUSHROOMS SHARE WITH LSD

There is no doubt that LSD is currently the most potent psychedelic drug. Thus, it can be considered a standard of measure when it comes to psychedelic effect. Any competitor must, therefore, measure up against it. Psilocybin is no exception.

What are the similarities between psilocybin and LSD?

Those who have never consumed magic mushrooms often wonder whether there is any similarity between psilocybin and LSD. This is probably because they would like to choose between the two. Mostly, it is consumers of LSD that are interested in knowing whether they can gain the same effect from magic mushrooms as an alternative.

Both psilocybin and LSD are:

- psychedelic substances – while there are differences in the kind of reactional behaviors that they cause to the consumer, both of them make the consumer feel 'high'.
- Fungal-based – both psilocybin and LSD are chemical compounds found in fungi. LSD is found in the Ergot fungus, a common parasitic fungus that attaches itself to the rye grain stalk.
- Not addictive – unlike marijuana and such other 'high' substances, neither psilocybin nor LSD is addictive. This means that you can consume them without the fear of becoming their unwilling slave entrapped in their 'high' snare. This allows you the freedom of choice and flexibility.

Furthermore, should you find yourself in a situation or place where the magic mushroom is lacking, you won't get tormented by addictive craving that often accompanies hard drugs.

What makes psilocybin different from its LSD competitor

While there are similarities between psilocybin and LSD, there are striking differences that make it preferable to choose one over the other.

The following are the main differences:

- Psilocybin is a naturally-occurring substance while LSD is a synthetic substance
- While mushrooms are largely legal in most jurisdictions, LSD is illegal
- LSD acts instantly upon ingestion – right from the mouth. Psilocybin takes time to act after being ingested as it has to be converted into psilocin within the small intestines.
- LSD has no taste. Psilocybin has a disgusting taste
- The effect of LSD lasts for about 8 to 12 hours, while that of psilocybin lasts for between 6 and 8 hours.
- LSD liberates your individuality as it makes you experience internal happiness and joy. On the other hand, psilocybin brings spiritual connections between the individual and

nature. This is why, unlike LSD, the magic mushroom is largely used in religious and ritualistic ceremonies.

- LSD has less of a hallucinating effect than psilocybin. While LSD increases mental focus and intensity on objects, thus bringing more clarity to their details, psilocybin distorts the clarity by virtually altering the image details such as color, shape, motion, etc. Thus, consumers of LSD won't experience static objects acquiring motion while consumers of psilocybin will more likely see stationary objects moving. Hence while LSD enhances the clarity of reality, psilocybin alters that reality.

HOW PSILOCYBIN WORKS TO ACHIEVE ITS PHANTASTICA

While ants get quickly satiated from eating psilocybin, humans get 'high' instead. How? This is because of the secondary compound that psilocybin is converted into – psilocin.

The conversion of psilocybin into psilocin

When you ingest psilocybin, it gets converted in the small intestines to psilocin. The psilocin gets transported into the brain through the bloodstream after absorption.

Psilocin mimics the brain's serotonin, a hormone responsible for the 'feel-good' effect.

How it affects the brain function

By mimicking serotonin, psilocin not only makes you 'feel good' but also distorts your perception and alters your thoughts and mood while maintaining your lucid awareness.

In a neurological sense, psilocin doesn't really 'mimic' serotonin but acts as its trigger.

The serotonin trigger

Psilocin acts as a brain receptor that triggers the release of serotonin from synaptic vesicles of neurons. Serotonin is a chemical responsible for the 'feel-good' effect. Thus, there is a change in mood, and you start feeling happier and more satisfied with life.

Low levels of serotonin are associated with negative moods, stress, anxiety, and even depression. By boosting serotonin levels, psilocin helps to relieve these symptoms and thus remedy these conditions.

The neural avalanche

You've probably seen or watched an avalanche taking place. It is a sudden massive movement of earth debris. Imagine the same happening with neurons! Yes, that's what happens when you start seeing the earn moving under your feet, objects changing colors, and transforming shapes, among other perceptive distortions that happen when the magic mushroom ferries you to the phantastica havens.

Behind this perceptive distortion, there is massive activation of the neurons. It is like a set of switches shutting one after another in rapid succession, thus creating a switch-on domino effect. This is what brings up a 'lighted moment' characterized by intense awareness. In this state, you begin to see things with much clarity that were hitherto hidden in the subconscious mind. Different 'dark rooms' of thoughts are 'lighted up' like an entire city being instantly lighted up such that sections that were previously invisible due to darkness instantly becomes visible.

In the brain's case, there is increased coordination and synchronization of the different functions of the brain, and the dark curtain that separates different sections of the brain seems to be suddenly broken such that the brain functions a one holistic system function towards one common end. This synergetic illumination increases the intensity of focus and the depth of concentration on that which is being perceived.

2

THERAPEUTIC BENEFITS OF PSILOCYBIN

Psychedelic mushrooms are distinguished for their therapeutic benefits. This is because they possess psilocybin.

They magically break your mental shackles, nurture your oneirogenic fantasies, and raise your entheogenic spirits, among other therapeutic benefits.

BREAKING THE MENTAL SHACKLES

Have you ever felt imprisoned in your mind? Have you ever felt that no matter how you try to free yourself from a certain set of thoughts or ways of thinking, you still find yourself trapped?

Our minds, like computers, operate based on a set program. This program, commonly referred to as the mindset, runs in a rather predetermined way. Thus, the only way to have a new way of thinking, a new kind of mental freedom, a new set of thoughts flowing is to reprogram your mindset.

Drawing from our computer analogy, however good a program is, if the CPU is limited, the program cannot achieve its optimal function. The CPU is nothing but a circuit of carefully wired logic gates. The same is the case with the brain. The brain circuitry, though much more complex, works similarly as the CPU. To radically alter the way this circuitry works, then it has to be rewired.

Hence, to break the mental shackles, there are two things you must do:

- Rewire the brain circuitry
- Reprogram your mindset

Psilocybin works on brain circuitry. It reconnects the disconnected parts. It creates newer and better connections that need to speed up certain functions.

Once this rewiring is done, your brain is supercharged. This way, it becomes easy for you to discover new opportunities to create better programs. This works the same way the computer world works. When a more powerful CPU is created, this creates an opportunity for more sophisticated software programs.

NURTURING YOUR ONEIROGENIC FANTASIES

Oneirogenic substances are those substances that 'create' dreams. Oneirogenic mushrooms enable you to enter the dream world while still in a state of consciousness. You can experience your lucid dreams intermingled with the real world to form a new reality.

The magnificence of this oneirogenic experience can be greatly appreciated when you are suffering from bad moods, depression, and such low moments. The magic mushrooms simply lift you beyond the clouds of depression and dampened spirit such that you can isolate yourself from the traps of negative experiences.

SOARING YOUR SPIRIT TO ITS PHANTASTICA 'NIRVANA'

Nirvana is a Buddhist term for a world where there is no suffering. It is a world where selfish desire is overcome.

Psilocybin mushroom brings that sense of connectedness to the nature of beings and the nature of things. Just as it brings the connectedness of the various brain parts and functions, it also brings connectedness of the various social relationships.

More than anything else, it brings that connectedness between our physical realms and spiritual realms such that we feel them co-existing synergistically within the same domain.

The boundary between heaven and earth diminishes as our minds transcend these physical limitations.

3

WHY MAGIC MUSHROOMS ARE IDEAL FOR YOU

Those who have taken a safe trip to the phantastica world of magics have never looked back. Not because they've become hopeless addicts, but because they've gained freedom unmatched elsewhere – the freedom to choose the best magic – and no choice has come close to a world in which the shroom's magic takes them.

You too can make a choice, a choice that you will never have to look back with regrets. It is a choice that you will be pleased to make every time and again.

Why? This is because magic mushrooms are ideal for you. We've already mentioned that they are non-addictive. Also, they are friendly to the brain, good for the moods, healthy to the body, and good for the appetite, among other great therapeutic benefits.

Let's explore these benefits, one-by-one…

THEY ARE NON-ADDICTIVE

The magic in the shrooms is one that liberates your mind. It is one that sets you free. It is not a magic that promises you heaven but takes you to an irreversible trip to hell. Those who repeatedly make this magic trip do so out of their own pleasant volition – not through compulsive addiction.

You can easily take a break from this joyous trip, disembark, and be earthly as you wait for the next trip. It is all your choice. It is all within your full uncompromised mental capacity.

THEY ARE GOOD FOR YOUR BRAIN

These shrooms magically supercharge your brain. They magically boost your brain capacity. Yet, this is no miracle. It is neuroscience at work.

Like an expert electrician, the psilocin repairs damaged brain circuitry, and it activates shut logic gates (the neurons). And like a system engineer, it synchronizes the various brain subsystems, thus optimizing their synergy as a giant holistic system.

We've already seen how psilocin acts as a serotonin trigger that brings forth a neural avalanche. This is the mechanism that supercharges your brain, making it gain supernatural powers.

You can creatively tap into this supernatural brain power to boost your performance and productivity while enjoying your phantastica nirvana. This is why psychedelic mushroom is loved by the creative minds at Silicon Valley. You don't have to be a geek at the Silicon Valley to tap into the secret of this marvelous potential. This book makes it no longer a secret.

THEIR SIDE EFFECT IS ONLY TEMPORARY

There is no perfect medicine. Every medicine has its unpleasant side. Psilocin also has its rather unpleasant side effect. However, this side effect, like that of other medicines, varies from person to person. It also varies from dose to dose.

Some experience nightmares instead of dreams on their trip. What the magic mushroom does is to magnify your mental imagery and accentuate the details. Thus, if your mind is packed up with negative images, trashes of negative experiences, and uncluttered remnants of a traumatic past, this is likely going to play on your mental reel like a movie. Scary! But, blending psilomagic with NLP, you can reprogram the meaning of these mental images so that, instead of them being scary, they become entertaining. You can also use NLP to detach these mental images from your mindset.

However, some experience an endless dose of sweet dreams on their trip. This is because they have a good pack of positive mental images, a great memory of past experiences, and positive future visions. This also plays on your mental reel like a movie. Sweet!

So, what you require to do is to declutter your mind. Get rid of those negative mental images. And discard the unwanted baggage so that your trip can be lighter, and thus you can soar higher to your phantastica nirvana.

Using techniques such as NLP, neuroplasticity, mindfulness meditation, creative visualization, positive thinking, and positive affirmation can be of great help. The good thing is that you can use these techniques to set the kind of experience you want to encounter on your magical trip.

The best of everything is that – everything has an end. Whether it is, pleasure or pain, it will be temporary. Thus, the side effects will also be temporary. This grants you unlimited opportunity to keep on fine-tuning your journey every other time you make the trip.

THEY BRING 'FEEL GOOD' EFFECT

Being a serotonin trigger, psilocybin mushrooms makes you feel happy, peaceful, and endowed with inner joy.

Why is serotonin such important?

To understand the important role that psilocybin plays by triggering serotonin, let's digest the important role played by serotonin itself.

Serotonin performs very important functions in the body. These include:

- Mood regulation – this is by far the most known function of serotonin.
- Bowel movement regulation – serotonin regulates bowel movement and other functions. It is also responsible for regulating appetite thus reducing your urge to over-eat
- Nausea – serotonin is responsible for creating nausea. Most

people would feel disgusted by this. However, feeling nauseating is a very important mechanism as it helps you expel toxins from the gut, thus saving your life. It can also work in a preventive way by stopping you from further consumption of toxic substances.

- Clotting – serotonin is released by blood platelets when you are wounded to increase blood clotting. Clotting reduces bleeding, which saves a life.

- Sexual regulation – just as serotonin reduces your appetite when you are full, it also reduces your libido to limit the sexual urge from becoming overwhelming.

- Sleep-wake cycle – serotonin plays an important role in regulating your sleep-wake cycle (circadian rhythm). This helps you have regular and stable sleep patterns.

Risks associated with low serotonin levels include:

- Low moods and behavioral compulsions
- Poor memory
- Anxiety and worries
- Aggression
- Low self-esteem
- Disturbed sleep patterns and insomnia
- Mental obsessions
- Panics and phobias
- Obesity and eating disorders
- Irritable bowel
- Chronic pain and migraines

- Drug abuse – especially alcohol

Looking at the risks associated with low serotonin levels, you can greatly appreciate the role psilocybin plays in mitigating them by simply boosting the serotonin levels.

THEY ARE NATURAL

Magic mushrooms are naturally-occurring ingredients. Their psilocybin is a naturally-occurring substance. Thus, unlike LSD, psilocybin is not artificially synthesized.

Being naturally-occurring means that they are less susceptible to the risk of artificial additives or reagents during the synthesizing process.

THEY ARE INEXPENSIVE

While the shelf price of LSD could be significantly lower due to pharmaceutical economies of scale, factoring the required capital outlay, the skills cost, and such other overhead costs, LSD cost is significantly higher than that of mushroom production.

Due to this low capital outlay, anyone with knowledge and keen interest such as you can be able to produce your mushroom. With this book, you have already acquired the knowledge - what awaits you is a keen interest, and you are ready to become a 'magic entrepreneur'.

THEY ARE THERAPEUTIC

What distinguishes psilocybin mushrooms from other edible mushrooms is its therapeutic benefits.

We have already seen how psilocin acts as a serotonin trigger. We have also seen the immense benefits of triggering serotonin.

Through this triggering mechanism, your moods are reset, your anxiety is wiped off, and your mental acuity is sharpened. You are no longer depressed, no longer dull, but joyful and happy.

Thus, the magic mushroom is the safest vessel that can easily ferry you on that therapeutic trip to the euphoric world.

THEY ARE NUTRITIONAL!

A lot of emphases is placed on the magic behind the psychedelic mushrooms, such that many people are dissuaded from remembering the nutritional benefits of these mushrooms.

The magic in psychedelic mushrooms does not steal away their nutritional value. Magic mushrooms are just as nutritional as any other mushroom, if not more.

Surprising nutritional facts:

- Cholesterol-free
- Fat-free
- Sodium-free
- Low-calorie

They are the best source of non-animal vitamin D. In fact, they continue accumulating vitamin D the more they are exposed to Sunlight during drying – probably the best reason why you should sun-dry them.

They are a rich source of minerals:

- Iron
- copper
- Potassium
- Phosphorous
- Selenium

Although nutritional content varies from species to species and the growth environment, generally, mushrooms possess the following nutritional content (per cup, or 70g):

- Protein: 2.2g
- Carbohydrates: 2.3g
- Calories: 15
- Sugars: 1.4g
- Fiber: 0.7g

As you can see, with magic shrooms, your trip to the mystic world is powered by a healthy dose of vitality.

II

HOW TO GROW YOUR FAVORITE PSYLOCYBIN MUSHROOMS

Psychedelic mushrooms marooning a tree trunk.

There is nothing that raises your passion for gardening than the memorable moments of euphoric trips you make to the phantastica world.

The best way to keep living these trip experiences is to have a steady supply of magic shrooms. Markets can fail. The only surety that you have against market failures is to grow your shrooms close to your hood.

In this Part, I am going to show you how to grow your favorite psilocybin mushrooms so that you are guaranteed of optimal yield in the most efficient way using tools and materials within your reach.

TOPICS COVERED

- **Why** you need to grow your own psilocybin mushrooms
- **Where** to grow your psychedelic mushrooms
- **How** to grow your magic mushrooms

4

WHY YOU NEED TO GROW YOUR OWN PSILOCYBIN MUSHROOMS

Many regular users of magic mushrooms prefer to grow it rather than become dependent on the market supply that is prone to failure.

Some of the factors that such users consider include risks of international trade, quality considerations, and boosting essential gardening skills through a hobby.

Let's explore each of these factors, and they make it imperative for you to keep your magic garden.

TO OVERCOME THE RISKS OF INTERNATIONAL TRADE

Imports are more susceptible to trade wars, hot wars, tariffs, bans, and international politics. This means that you can easily find that your favorite magic is no longer available.

To avoid this potential scarcity plus other costs and inconveniences, it is necessary for you to grow your magic to ensure continued supply without running the risks of geopolitical disruptions.

To ensure that you have an adequate supply

Even if the source of your magic is not sourced internationally, local supplies can also get disrupted. Growing your magic does not necessarily mean that you will be immune to supply shocks and shortages, but you will have diversified sourcing options, thus reducing the risks.

To ensure that you are in control of its natural growth process

In most places, psychedelic mushrooms are imported. This means that they have taken ages to arrive at your convenience store.

Furthermore, they are likely going to have nutritional and therapeutic compromises. This is especially if you like taking them fresh.

Imported mushrooms are heavily mechanized and a lot often, are grown unnaturally. This compromises the potency of their magic plus their nutritional value. Furthermore, the storage and transport facilities could be contaminated, especially by heavy metals, thus increasing your risk of a toxic ingestion.

The best way to make sure that their nutritional value is guaranteed plus their magic potency remains undiluted. You have to be in control of their growth process.

To keep yourself busy and occupied with your shroom hobby

There no environmental activity that is as therapeutic as gardening. With gardening, you not only engage in physical activity but also relieve yourself from mental stress and potential depression. Even before the magic matures enough to work on your brain, the activity itself has already started working on it.

A hobby that helps you take care of nature, improve your nutrition, and reduce hunger is such a noble hobby. Your shroom garden is not just a garden but a spiritual sanctuary. Tend to this mycological garden, and you will find your energy flow being harmoniously synchronized with that of nature.

5

WHERE TO GROW YOUR PSYCHEDELIC MUSHROOMS

The biggest question that faces urban dwellers is where to grow their magic mushrooms.

With the developed world comprising of almost 80% urban dwellers, it happens that most shroom consumers are urban dwellers. Yet, it is them that need to guarantee themselves of consistent supply, therapeutic potency, and nutritional value from their beloved magic.

Surprisingly, there is plenty of space within the urban dwellings where the magic mushrooms can easily grow and flourish.

I am not inventing a new space within your habitat but simply reminding you to look around and see it. There is enough space to grow your magic indoors... and, for some of you, there is still some space to grow your shrooms outdoors.

GROWING MAGIC INDOORS

Growing psychedelic mushrooms indoors is the most popular way for urban dwellers, maybe because people don't have enough space outdoors. Or, maybe because they want to keep privacy from prying eyes – especially, in grey-area jurisdictions where the magic is criminalized or simply not acceptable.

Nonetheless, whichever the case, and for whatever reason you may have, let's explore indoor spaces where you can puff in your magic.

Free room

If you have a small free room, this could be the best option. This is because, apart from controlling the light, you can also easily control the temperature and access. You can also be able to control the overall humidity.

A free room also allows you maximum creativity as to whether you want to have shelves, grounded bags, or even hanging bags for growing your shrooms.

Corridor & Verandah

If you have no free or suitable room, you can take advantage of the corridor or veranda. However, if you have no strict control over the access to the corridor/veranda, then you will need to have a cupboard-like or shelf enclosure so that other people have no direct access to your shrooms.

Balcony

A balcony is an ideal place, especially if it is exclusive to your house. Thus, you can control the movement in and out of the balcony. Furthermore, you can easily and partially enclose a part of the balcony so that it becomes like a small room. In case you don't want to enclose partially, you can still use the balcony just as you would do with the corridor and verandah.

Attic/loft

Attic/Loft is a great place to grow your shrooms. The loft is a room within the attic. Instead of using the entire attic (the space below the roof), you can partition it into lofts. This way, you can have a grow room, a materials/tools room, and even your restroom after hard work.

Garage

If you have a big garage space that is rarely used, you can make a small enclosure out of it and use it as a planting site for your shrooms.

GROWING YOUR MAGIC SHROOMS OUTDOORS

Growing mushrooms outdoor is not the recommended way as you have limited control over the growing conditions. Mushrooms grown outdoors tend to take longer to mature. Since you have limited control over their growth condition, you cannot afford to accelerate their growth rate as you would do with indoor mushrooms.

Also, their productivity is often lower as the mushroom becomes more susceptible to the vagaries of weather.

However, if you have no indoor space, then, this remains the only option left. Some of the outdoor places where you can grow your shroom include the kitchen garden, grass shade, tree trunk, fence canopy, valley cave, among others.

Kitchen garden

The kitchen garden can be a nice place to plant your shrooms. The advantage of a kitchen garden is that you can use the kitchen garden to prepare compost for your shrooms as well as partition a small space to plant the shrooms.

Grass shade

Like a car shade, you can create a shade made of grass. The purpose of the grass is to prevent strong light and also create a damp environment where you can grow your shrooms. Grass can also act as a medium through which you can humidify the mushroom growing space.

Tree trunk

A rotting tree trunk is ideal for certain species of psilocybin mushrooms. Also, only certain trees can provide the substrate medium. Thus, while this can work, it is pretty challenging and requires first-hand knowledge of the tree species for the substrate and the mushroom species for the growth. Furthermore, the tree trunk is less ideal in urban setup than in rural setup.

Fence canopy

Certain hedge fences can easily provide a canopy plus humus that promotes the growth of fungi. You need to know the kind of trees/shrubs that can provide the required canopy and humus.

Valley cave

If you reside in a place that has rugged terrain, then, you can easily find some cave in a valley. This is an ideal place to plant those shroom species that easily grow in partially enclosed underground. If there is no cave, you can easily dig one for this purpose.

However, this is ideal in a rural setup as it is hard to find such terrain or such a space in an urban setup.

6

HOW TO GROW YOUR MAGIC MUSHROOMS

Now that you have decided where to grow your shrooms, the next thing is to know how to grow them in your chosen place.

The first thing to do is to decide on what is going to be your planting material. Once you choose your preferred planting material, you can then be able to determine the kind of substrate that is ideal for your planting material.

Having chosen the right substrate for your material, you can go ahead and prepare it. The substrate will require to be held in a container for planting. Container that holds the substrate should be ideal for your chosen planting site.

But before you embark on growing your mushroom, you must understand the entire lifecycle of your mushroom so that you can be able to tell with certainty at what stage of growth your mushroom is experiencing.

UNDERSTAND THE MUSHROOM LIFECYCLE

Understanding the mushroom lifecycle makes you get prepared for your mushroom's next stage of growth.

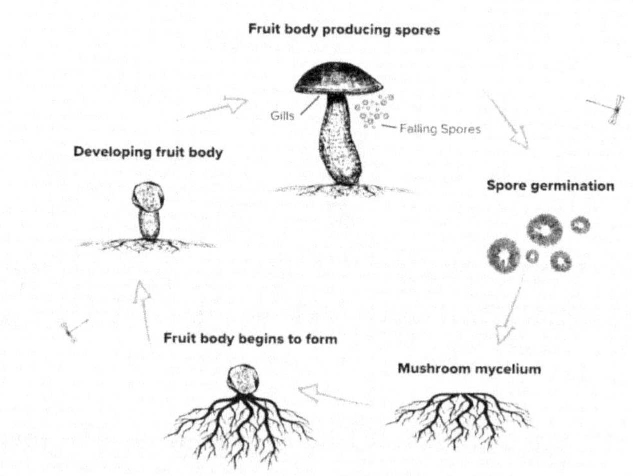

Image source: libreshot.com

The mushroom lifecycle - Image source: nicepng.com

Without going into the seed-and-fruit-question as to what came first, let's avoid this controversy by beginning with the fruit (fruit body) as depicted in the above diagram.

The cap (fruit body) has gills beneath it. The gills, when mature, are populated with **spores** just as pollen grains in a petal. These pores appear as brownish micro-granules. The pattern they form on the gills is called **spore print**.

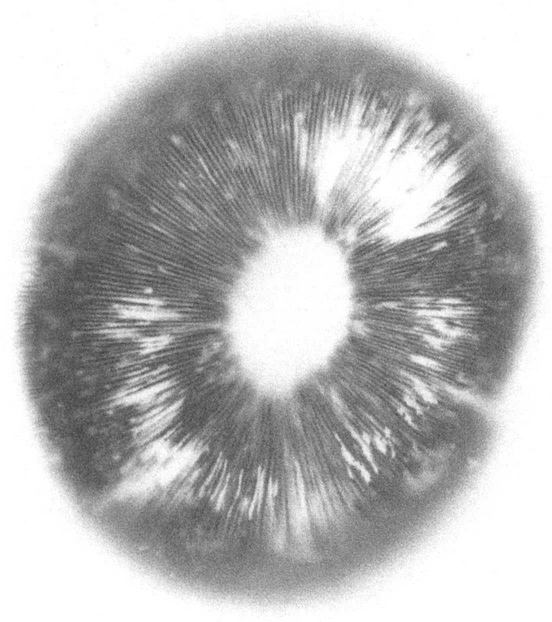

Spore prints.

Photo by Ranko /CC BY 3.0

After a while, the spores start falling on the ground. If you use a magnifying lens, you can easily observe them on the ground when fallen. If you want to prepare your own culture, before the gills open up, you place on the ground tinfoil that not only covers the cap's circumference but extends some few centimeters beyond just to capture those spores dispersed farther by the wind.

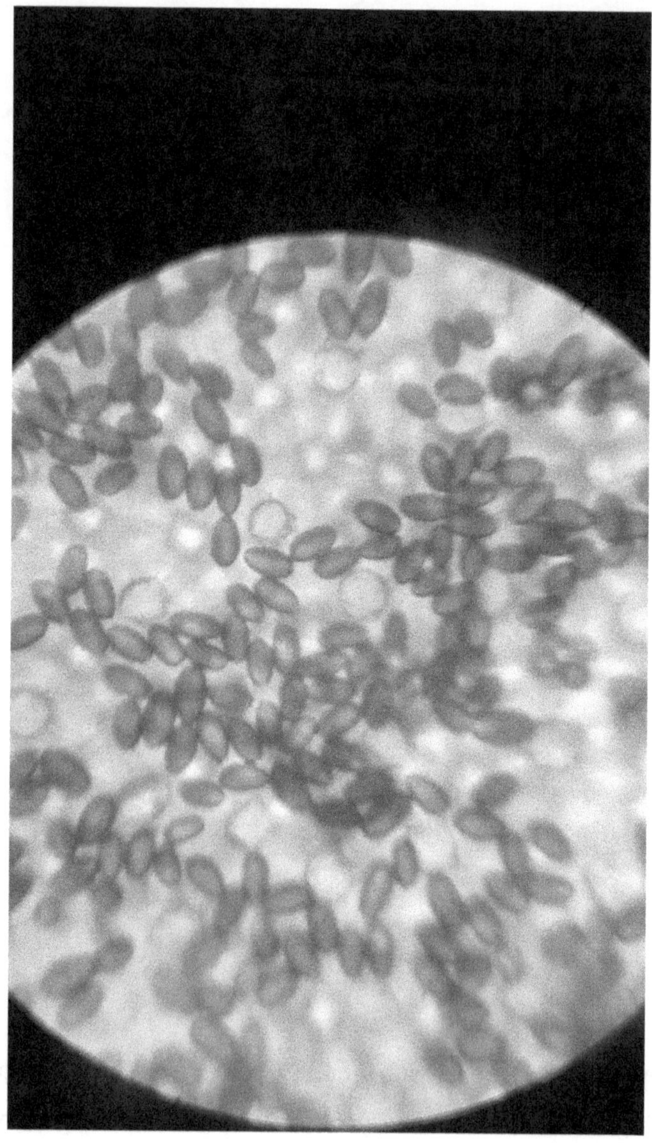

Spores on a glass slate observed through a magnifying lens
Photo by Chris /CC BY 4.0

The spores germinate **hyphae**. A hypha is just like a bud on a germinating seed. However, unlike buds, they are simply sexually-active organs. Compatible hyphae mate to form fertilized **mycelium**. Mycelium appears as a white root-like network of fiber.

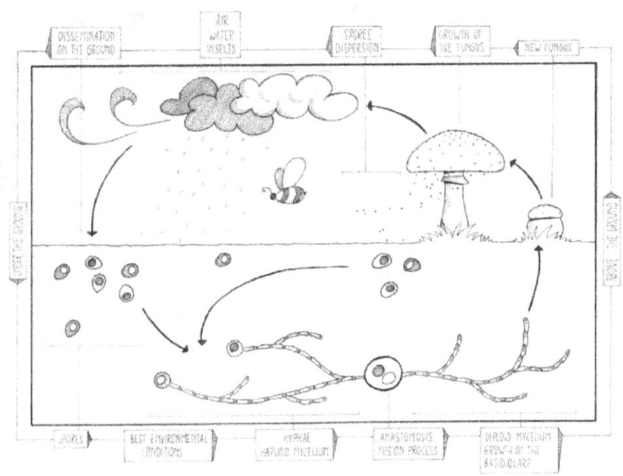

Mushroom sexual reproduction lifecycle (from spores to mycelium)
Photo by Anita Righetto, DensityDesign Research Lab /CC BY 4.0

Mycelium expands to form a **mycelium colony** on the substrate. This expansion is what we call colonization, and it occurs during the incubation period (3-4 weeks, in a controlled environment).

Hyphae on the ground – early stages of expansion
Photo by TheAlphaWolf /CC BY 3.0

On the surface, the mycelium colony can appear as white meshed threads holding the surface. These threads can sew together lumps of debris. However, the threads are too weak to resist the braking force of your hand.

A fully-formed Mycelium colony

Photo by Lex /CC BY-SA 3.0

After colonization, mycelium condenses into **hyphal knots**. Hyphal knots are tiny growth lumps. The **hyphal knot** develops into **primordia**.

A primordium is a baby mushroom. It appears as a pin-like formation, which eventually protrudes to form the mushroom cap.

Mushroom primordia

Photo by Wendell Smith /CC BY 2.0

To honor Charles Darwin's theory of survival for the fittest, natural selection occurs such that only the fittest primordium in a cluster is left to continue growing while those that are not fit or have low chances of survival are left to die. Eventually, the dead become humus for the surviving ones.

The fittest primordium gets enough space and nutrients to grow into a fruiting body. After a short while, the fruiting matures into a full mushroom ready for heavens (harvest!). To the Psilonauts, this fully-grown blossom is nature's beckoning call to transcendent heavens. The ecstatic expectancy is filled with pregnant fantasies of psilonautic trips to the worlds beyond.

Well, we are still here in the garden. To complete the lifecycle, the proudly brave mushroom stands out fully occupying its domain. If you've got to pick, just do it tenderly. Don't brutalize its pride. And just pick enough for your trip. If there is more to share, do share with others. You can also become a shroompreneur (shrooms entrepreneur) by selling them for profit.

A fully-grown **Amanita muscaria** standing tall

Photo by JJ Harrison /GFDL

Out of the dream into reality, let's go planting...

DECIDE ON YOUR PREFERRED PLANTING MATERIAL

To get the right planting material, you have to decide on the mushroom species that you want to get its magic from.

There are two options when it comes to planting material:

- Spores
- Spawns

You can use spores if you are more experienced with growing mushrooms and you can easily access mature mushrooms whereby you can be able to tap their falling spores.

However, if you are a newbie, the best option is to use spawns which come in the form of grow-kits.

The grow-kits have a ready-made culture. This culture comprises a substrate that is already colonized by mycelium and thus all you need is to break the substrate into pieces that you can use to inoculate the secondary substrate.

THE VARIOUS SPECIES OF PSILOCYBIN MUSHROOMS TO CHOOSE FROM

There are almost 200 species of psilocybes. Thus, it would be daunting to list and describe all of them in this book. Nonetheless, we are going to consider the most common types of psilocybes.

The following are the top (7) species of psilocybes that you can consider:

1. *Psilocybe cubensis (Stropharia cubensis)*

Psilocybe cubensis is probably the most common of all psilocybe species. It is found in most tropical lands – from Asia to Africa and the Americas.

main features

Cap (pileus):

- Shape – conic (pagoda-shaped) while young. Flat or convex while aged.
- Color – reddish-cinnamon when young and golden-brown when aged.
- Width - 2-9cm
- Texture – smooth. Slimy when moist.

Gills (Lamella):

- Color – whitish at first. Turns purple-grey upon maturity and then black as it ages.

- Veil – deep purple
- Spore print – dark-brown or purple

Stipe (Stem/stalk):

- Color – white-yellowish. Manifests blue hue when bruised or aged.
- Length – 4-15cm
- Thickness – 4-14mm
- Ring (annulus) – white ring

Spores (when deposited):

- Color – brown to dark purple.
- Shape – elongated ellipsoid
- Size - 11.5–17 x 8–11 micrometers

Potency:

- Psilocybin – 0.63%
- Psilocin – 0.60%
- Baeocystin – 0.025%

Strains:

- Golden teacher
- Huautla
- Penis Envy

- Blue Meanie
- B+ Cubensis
- PF Classic
- Z Strain
- Orissa India
- Cambodian
- Alacabenzi
- Florida White (F+)
- Many more…

Habitat:

- Substrate - highly versatile and adaptable. However, straw, Brown Rice Flower (BRF), Psilocybe Fanaticus Technique (PF-Tek), rye grain, and manure are commonly used for psilocybe cubensis cultivation.
- Location – tropics and sub-tropics

The most distinct feature(s):

- Thick, dense stems
- Large, broad caps

Psilocybe cubensis

Photo by Zergboy / Wikimedia

Psilocybe cubensis is highly versatile and can adapt to different climatic conditions and substrates. This makes it ideal for beginners and is often their first choice.

2. Psilocybe cyanescens

Known for its distinct wavy cap, psilocybe cyanescens is a native of North America. It has one of the highest levels of potency, as it contains about 0.85% psilocybin.

main features

Cap (pileus):

- Shape – rounded and closed around the stem while young. Broadly opens up to a convex shape when adult.
- Color – chestnut brown to caramel when young (or fresh). Yellowish-brown when aged (or dry)
- Width - 1.5–5 cm
- Texture – smooth. Slimy when moist.
- Umbo – the remains in place even as the cap turns convex. It becomes depressed with wavy margins upon maturity.

Gills (Lamella):

- Color – pale tan at the start. cinnamon-smoky brown upon full maturity.
- Spore print – dark-brown or purple

Stipe (Stem/stalk):

- Color – whitish. Manifests blue hue when bruised or aged.
- Length – 2-8cm
- Thickness – 2-5mm
- Ring (annulus) –
- Volva – silky. Covered with rhizomorphs (white mycelial tufts)
- Shape – slightly curved. Thicker towards the base.

Spores (when deposited):

- Color – brown to dark purple.
- Shape – elongated ellipsoid
- Size - 9-12 x 5-8 micrometers

Potency:

- Psilocybin – 0.85%
- Psilocin – 0.36%
- Baeocystin – 0.03%

Strains:

- N/A

Habitat:

- Substrate - decaying wood matter.
- Location – North America

The most distinct feature(s):

- Wavy cap
- Undulating edges

Psilocybe cyanescens
Photo by Caleb Brown / CC BY-SA 3.0

3. *Psilocybe stuntzii*

Nicknamed Stuntz's Blue legs and Blue Ringers, Psilocybe stuntzii is a rare species of magic mushrooms.

This mushroom has a characteristic sticky, brownish cap with brownish gills and brownish, ringed stalk.

main features

Cap (pileus):

- Shape – rounded and closed around the stem while young. Broadly opens up to a convex shape when adult. Slightly wavy and uplifted when adult.
- Color – dark to yellow-brown. Green-tinged on the margins
- Width - 1.5 - 4 cm

- Texture – smooth. Sticky when moist.
- Umbo – the remains in place even as the cap turns convex.

Gills (Lamella):

- Color – whitish at first. Turns purple-grey upon maturity and then black as it ages.
- Veil – bluish veil
- Spore print – dark-brown or purple

Stipe (Stem/stalk):

- Color – Yellowish
- Length – 3-6 cm
- Thickness – 3mm
- Ring (annulus) – membranous ring
- Volva – smooth to fibrous
- Shape – Thicker towards the base.

Spores (when deposited):

- Color – brown to dark purple.
- Shape – elongated ellipsoid. Pore at the tip
- Size - 8-12.5 X 6-8 micrometers

Potency(%):

- Psilocybin – 0.36%

- Psilocin – 0.12%
- Baeocystin – 0.02%

Strains:

- N/A

Habitat:

- Substrate – coniferous wood-chip mulch
- Location – Pacific North-West

The most distinct feature(s):

- Sticky cap
- Ringed stalk

Psilocybe stuntzii
Photo by Caleb Brown / CC BY-SA 3.0

4. Psilocybe azurescens

Fondly referred to as 'flying saucer' due to the shape of its cap once fully mature, psilocybe azurescens is the most potent of the known psilocybes.

A native of Oregon and Washington States in the US, psilocybe is very popular with outdoor growers.

main features

Cap (pileus):

- Shape – conic while young. Flat or convex while aged.
- Color – ochraceous brown. Pitted with dark blue or bluish-black zones when aged.
- Width - 3-10cm
- Texture – smooth. Viscous when moist.
- Umbo – nipple-like. Remains in place even as the cap turns convex or flat.
- Pellicle – colorless.

Gills (Lamella):

- Color – brownish
- Veil – bluish
- Spore print –purple-brown

Stipe (Stem/stalk):

- Color – silky white. Turns dingy-brown when aged.
- Length – 9-20cm
- Thickness – 3-6mm
- Ring (annulus) – bluish
- Volva – dingy-brown. Covered with rhizomorphs (white mycelial tufts)
- Shape – slightly curved. Thicker towards the base.

Spores (when deposited):

- Color – brown to dark purple.

- Shape – elongated ellipsoid
- Size - 11.5–17 x 8–11 micrometers

Potency:

- Psilocybin – 1.78%
- Psilocin – 0.38%
- Baeocystin – 0.35%

Strains:

- N/A

Habitat:

- Substrate - decaying wood matter, cow mulch, grass with high lignin content.
- Location – Oregon and Washington States in the US

The most distinct feature(s):

- 'Flying-saucer' cap
- Highest potency level.
- Outdoor cultivation

Psilocybe azurescens

Photo by Shroom360 / CC BY-SA 3.0

5. Psilocybe Mexicana

Popularly known as 'the flesh of gods', Psilocybe Mexicana is aboriginal species of South America. It was traditionally used by the Aztech people for religious and spiritual purposes, thus deriving its nickname 'the flesh of gods'. Mexico is believed to be its ancestral home. However, it has extended its tentacles into Guatemala and Costa Rica.

main features

Cap (pileus):

- Shape – conic at the start. Convex at maturity
- Color –brown to ocherous when young. Beige to straw when aged.
- Width – 0.5–3 cm
- Texture – smooth. Viscid when moist.
- Umbo – small size

Gills (Lamella):

- Color – grey to purple-brown. Whitish edges.
- Veil – thinly fibrillose
- Spore print – dark purple-brown

Stipe (Stem/stalk):

- Color – Yellowish to brownish. Darkens with age.
- Length – 4-10cm
- Thickness – 1-3mm
- Ring (annulus) – reddish-brown flesh
- Volva – silky. Covered with rhizomorphs (white mycelial tufts)
- Shape – Uniform thickness, or narrower towards the base.

Spores (when deposited):

- Color – dark purplish brown

- Shape – ellipsoid (side view) and subrhomboid (face view)
- Size – 8-9.9 x 5.5-7.7 micrometers

Potency:

- Psilocybin – 0.25%
- Psilocin – 0.15%
- Baeocystin – 0.02%

Strains:

- N/A

Habitat:

- Substrate - grassy areas bordering deciduous forests, meadows, horse pastures.
- Location – Mexico, Guatemala, and Costa Rica

The most distinct feature(s):

- The stem is uniformly thick or slightly slender towards the base.
- Very small umbo

Psilocybe Mexicana
Photo by Alonso / CC BY-SA 3.0

Psilocybe Mexicana is known for its truffles or sclerotia. If you are a fan of munching mushroom truffles, then the flesh of gods is a must-have in your mycological sanctuary.

6. *Psilocybe semilanceata*

Fondly known as 'Liberty cap' is one of the most liberally available psychedelic mushroom species. Despite its small size, Liberty cap is highly potent and can quicks send you packing on a trip to the mystic world.

main features

Cap (pileus):

- Shape – conic to obtusely conic. Rolled inwards while young. Unrolls outwards as it matures and even sometimes flattens or curls upwards.
- Color – dark chestnut brown when young (or fresh). Yellowish-brown when aged (or dry)
- Width - 0.5–2.5 cm
- Texture – smooth. Slimy when moist.
- Umbo – nipple-shaped
- Pellicle – viscid moist

Gills (Lamella):

- Color – brown at the start. Grey and then purplish-brown upon full maturity.
- Veil – cobweb-like partial veil
- Spore print – deep reddish purple-brown

Stipe (Stem/stalk):

- Color – Yellowish-brown
- Length – 4.5-14cm
- Thickness – 1-3.5mm

- Ring (annulus) – faded annular zone marks.
- Shape – flexuous and pliant. Thicker towards the base.

Spores (when deposited):

- Color – brown to dark purple.
- Shape –ellipsoidal
- Texture - smooth
- Size - 11-14 x 7-19 microns

Potency:

- Psilocybin – 0.98%
- Psilocin – 0.02%
- Baeocystin – 0.36%

Strains:

- N/A

Habitat:

- Substrate – sheep or cow dung, sedges (decaying root remains), highly organic wetlands
- Location – New Zealand, some parts of Europe (especially UK), Pacific North West.

The most distinct feature(s):

- Spear-shaped
- Rolled cap edges

Psilocybe semilanceata

Photo by Alan Rockefeller / CC BY-SA 3.0

Liberty cap does not shy away from growing liberally in the open fields, especially manured pasture. This is why it is generously available to psilonauts in many places in the world.

The distinctive feature of psilocybe semilanceata is its bell-shaped or conical shaped cap that is embellished with a nipple-like protrusion at its apex.

7. *Psilocybe baeocystis*

Known by the fond name of 'bluebells', psilocybe baeocystis has other names such as knobby tops, bottle caps, and olive caps. All these names describe the physical characteristics of the cap.

main features

Cap (pileus):

- Shape – conic to obtusely conic. Cap margins distinctly rippled and turned inwards.
- Color – dark olive-brown. Sometimes steel blue. Copper-brown towards the center when dried.
- Width - 1.5–5.5 cm
- Texture – smooth. Viscid when moist.
- Umbo – the remains in place even as the cap turns convex. It becomes depressed with wavy margins upon maturity.
- Pellicle – separable and gelatinous.

Gills (Lamella):

- Color – greyish or cinnamon brown with pallid edges
- Veil – evanescent partial veil
- Spore print – dark purplish-brown

Stipe (Stem/stalk):

- Color – pallid to brownish with a whitish filament. Yellowish towards the top
- Length – 5-7cm

- Thickness – 2-3mm
- Ring (annulus) – indistinguishable.
- Volva –Covered with rhizomorphs
- Shape – slightly curved. Thicker towards the base.
- Sturdiness - brittle

Spores (when deposited):

- Color –dark purplish-brown.
- Shape – ellipsoid (mango-like shape)
- Size - 9.5–13.7 x 5.5–6.6 micrometers

Potency:

- Psilocybin – 0.85%
- Psilocin – 0.59%
- Baeocystin – 0.01%

Strains:

- N/A

Habitat:

- Substrate - decaying wood matter (conifer mulch, wood chip, ground bark), peat moss, lawns, and pasture.
- Location – North America

The most distinct feature(s):

- Rippled edges
- Highly potent when fresh. Diminished potency when dry.

Psilocybe baeocystis
Photo by Caleb Brown / CC BY-SA 3.0

One unique feature of psilocybe baeocystiss that its potency is high when fresh and rapidly declines as it dries. Thus, this is a species that you have to munch while still fresh.

FACTORS DETERMINING YOUR CHOICE OF PSYCHEDELIC MUSHROOM

1. *Availability of the planting material*

The availability of planting material is very important. You may wish to plant a certain species, but if it is not available in shops within your reach, then, it will be difficult for you to be assured of the materials when you need them most.

The first task to do is to take an inventory of magic species available within your locality. In case there is a certain species that you want to grow but is not available within your locality, check whether you can order it online and the reliability of doing so.

2. *The potency of the species*

Different species of psychedelic mushrooms are endowed with different levels of psilocybin potency. Genetically, some are more potent than others.

3. *The survival versatility of the species*

If you are a beginner, you would like to improve the chances of your project coming to fruition. Thus, you would prefer a species that has a higher survival versatility – that is, it can easily survive under different environments and more constrained conditions.

Some species are extremely sensitive and less versatile. These are not for you if you are a beginner.

4. *Your taste and preferences*

Just like food mushrooms, magic mushrooms have different tastes. The best way to grow your preferred taste is to sample tastes of various species and find out the taste that you like.

You will be more motivated to cultivate that magic that pleasantly scintillates your taste buds than the one that scares them away. Nonetheless, you have to balance between taste and potency. Some species are tastier but less potent while others are more potent but bitter.

5. *Your growth environment*

What environment are you capable of providing for your shrooms? Different species have a unique environment that they flourish.

In consideration of the previous factors, go for a species which you can easily create a conducive environment for its growth, flourish, and fruition.

6. *Your experience*

Your experience matters. You can either be an experienced grower or consumer - or both.

If you are a very experienced grower, then, you easily manage the growth of most species of magic mushrooms. However, if you are less experienced, especially a beginner, then, you will go for a species that is less demanding in terms of growth and nurturing.

As an experienced consumer, you will grow species that have high potency for your consumption. However, if you are new to the consumption of psychedelic mushrooms, then, you are better off starting with less potent mushrooms that won't give you a difficult time consuming them. This is safe for your test-drive.

After successful test-drive, you can gradually shift gear to growing more potent mushrooms as you gain experience of handling more rugged terrains on your trips.

PREPARE THE SUBSTRATE

The substrate is the medium that provides nutrients, water, and support to the mycelium during the formative stages of the shroom and continues to provide a foundation for the growth to maturity of the shroom.

Without the substrate, the mushroom will simply not grow. Thus, the substrate has a huge impact on the survivability, growth, and productivity of the shrooms. This is why you have to select the right substrate material and prepare it well.

SELECTING THE RIGHT SUBSTRATE MATERIAL

There are many substrate materials to choose from. Factors that will determine your substrate material are:

1. *Quality*

Quality of the substrate material is important when it comes to survivability and growth of your shrooms. Qualitative factors include permeability, hydration, and aeration.

Permeability refers to the ability of the material to allow moisture to move within its membrane.

Hydration refers to the ability of the material to absorb and keep moisture. Mushrooms require a lot of moisture to grow and flourish.

Aeration refers to the ability of the material to easily allow air to circulate. A material with poor aeration will easily cause decay of the mycelium instead of growth.

The substrate material should be permeable, allows high levels of hydration and fairly aerated.

2. *Availability*

Availability of the preferred material is important, especially if you plan to grow shrooms on a large-scale and in the long-term. A material that is not easily available with frustrate your success.

Do basic research in your local market to establish the availability of the various potential materials for your shrooms to find out how easily available each material is. This will help you select the most appropriate material.

3. *Fitness for space*

While fitness for space may not be such a big factor when you have grinders, it can be a factor in case you don't. When you are operating on a small, non-commercial scale, you need a material that can easily fit within your tiny space – e.g. within a gunny bag, within a drawer or even a small container.

Grains, sawdust, and such other granulated materials can easily fit into small containers. Straws, logs, and such other long fibers will require to be trimmed or ground.

4. *Cost*

How expensive is your preferred material? It would be necessary for the cost to be economical. You would not like to go for materials that will make the cost of growing your shrooms much higher than the price of buying the same shrooms in the market.

5. *The shroom species*

Naturally, different species do well on certain specific substrates. Some species do well on dead logs while others do well on straws. Still, others do well on powdery substrates. The best substrate is that which mimics the natural characteristics of a species' preferred substrate.

However, this should not limit you as most shroom species are tolerant of the commonly used substrates such as straws, grains, sawdust, and such like.

Substrate material

There are many substrate materials to choose from. The following are the most widely used substrate materials:

- Agar
- Grains (brown rice grain, brown wheat grain, popcorns, etc.)
- Straws (rye straws, wheat straws, etc.)
- Coir
- Sawdust
- Woodchips/cardboard chips
- Paper pellets

- Hardwood pellets
- Manure

Substrate supplements

Substrate supplements are those compounds that boost the efficacy of the substrate. Common substrate materials include:

- Gypsum (calcium sulfate)
- Lime (calcium carbonate)
- Yeast
- Malt extracts
- Coffee grounds

Treating your substrate

Shrooms are very sensitive to contamination. The contaminants could be physical, chemical, or biological. In most cases, when it comes to the treatment of a substrate, it is to get rid of biological contaminants such as pests, parasites, and disease-causing micro-organisms.

Decontaminating the substrate

Decontamination is the most common treatment of substrates. The following are the two methods that you can use to decontaminate your substrate:

- Pasteurization
- Sterilization

PASTEURIZING YOUR SUBSTRATE

Pasteurization refers to minimizing the amount of micro-organism in the substrate so that they do not outcompete the mycelium in growth.

Different substrate materials will require a slightly different approach to sterilization. However, the common denominator is that you boil the substrate in water or steam it at between 160- and 180-degrees Fahrenheit.

STERILIZING YOUR SUBSTRATE

Unlike pasteurization that helps to minimize the bad bacteria while sparing good bacteria, sterilization is about killing all micro-organisms – whether good or bad.

The primary difference between the pasteurization approach and the sterilization approach is the temperature. For sterilization, the temperature is put to the extreme provided that the substrate material is not damaged. Typically, sterilization temperate is set above 250 degrees Fahrenheit.

GET THE SUBSTRATE CONTAINER READY

You can use wooden containers, plastic containers, ceramic containers, and even metallic containers.

The container preparation

Container preparation involves the following steps:

1. Get the right size of container that fits your space layout and the container holder
2. Disinfect the container using a sterilizer such as a hydrogen peroxide, bleach, or 99% isopropyl alcohol. In the case of a metallic container, avoid using bleach or hydrogen peroxide as they can react with the metals to form dangerous acids or compounds.
3. Dry and desiccate the container
4. Encase/insulate the container

Casing

Casing the substrate happens after filling the substrate container but before closing the 'lid'.

Why casing?

The following are the main reasons that make it imperative to case your substrate:

- Protection against rapid evaporation
- Hydrating the substrate
- Conditioning the substrate for pinhead formation
- Providing a conducive environment for beneficial micro-organisms

Casing materials

The material used for casing include:

- Vermiculite
- Perlite
- Peat moss
- Water crystals

Container decontaminants

The following are decontaminants that you can use for containers:

- Isopropyl alcohol
- Hydrogen peroxide
- Paraffin
- Bleach

Materials & tools used for decontamination purposes:

- Surgical hand gloves
- Masks
- Aluminum foil

The container holder

A container holder is any object that holds the container into the right space. This could be a shelf, a hanger, a raised ground platform, or any other holder.

The shelf

A shelf is a great holder for your containers. However, you can still use the shelf as a container by itself. I prefer using the shelf as a holder rather than a container.

Disinfect the wooden shelves using bleach or hydrogen peroxide, or 70% isopropyl alcohol. This will ensure that molds and other micro-organisms on the shelf's surface do not spread into the substrate.

The tray

Trays are great if you love the portability. With a tray, you can easily move the substrate from one site to another. However, make sure that you do not expose your shrooms to contamination while moving the tray from one point to another. Ideally, only move the tray from one spot to another within the secured and decontaminated site.

Trays on the shelf

My best choice is to place the trays on the movable shelf. This allows me to maximize maneuverability.

Hangers on the beam

Hangers are good when your substrate or grow-medium is an elongated plastic bag.

Straight metallic (or wooden) horizontal beams are fixed about 4 feet above the ground (depending on the length of the bags) across the room. These rounded beams can be 2-3 feet apart depending on the diameter of the bags.

These grow bags are placed on a hanger and then the hanger is placed on the beam. The hangers can be spaced about 1.5-2 feet apart depending on the diameter of the bags.

Thus, the shrooms will grow on the cylindrical surface of the bags which already have holes poked for the sprouts.

Raised ground platform

For a very heavy substrate, especially for heavy commercial farming, the ideal container holder is a raised ground platform. The raised platform is necessary where the ground is outdoor but enclosed by a tent or other temporary arrangement.

If indoors, provided that the floor is cemented, you may not need a raised floor. However, just to avoid accidental flooding that could soak the substrate, you can have a raised platform as a matter of precaution. The raised platform is also ideal in case you have rows with substrate placed in gunny bags such that the mushrooms shoot from the top and sideways.

CULTURE THE SPORES

When it comes to a culture for the spores, you can either acquire ready-made culture, or you can make your own culture.

Acquiring ready-made culture

If you are a beginner, it is preferable to acquire a ready-made culture. If a friend can donate to you, well and good, otherwise, you can easily buy ready-made culture from the shroom shops.

Preparing your own culture

In case you are not going to buy a ready culture (in a grow-kit), you will have to prepare your own culture. This involves fetching the spores and then germinating them on the base substrate.

Fetching the spores

You will need to harvest the spores from the already fruited shrooms. You will need to lay on the ground a medium that will collect the falling spores from the shroom grills. A tissue paper can easily work as the medium for collecting these spores.

Germinating the spores on the base substrate

Once you have collected the spores, you can then prepare them for germination.

SET THE PLANTING SITE

The planting site should be secure, of the right temperate, humidified, and with controlled lighting.

Securing the site

Security is paramount if you want your shrooms to give you optimal yield. You need to secure your shrooms against:

- Unauthorized people – people who are not authorized to access your magic shrine should be kept off. Children are always curious and will be tempted to dig up the substrate, poke holes in it, or even try to pick the sprouts. Both children and adults can infect the site with micro-organisms that may end up harming the mushrooms.

- Pets – pets will not only do the kind of harm that curious children would do, but they could also contain more dangerous micro-organisms than humans.
- Parasites – rodents are the most dangerous big parasites to the shrooms. Apart from rodents such as rats and mice, insects such as ants and worms can cause harm to the shrooms by feeding on them.

To secure the site:

- Enclose it
- Control movements into and out of the enclosure
- Spray the close environs with pesticides
- If the ground is not cemented, raise the platform upon which the substrate and containers are stood on.

Setting the right temperature

Different species require slightly different temperatures to grow and flourish. Furthermore, different stages of growth require different temperatures. However, irrespective of the species, the following are general ranges:

- Incubation period - 28-30°C
- Pinhead formation period - 22-24 °C
- Cropping period - 22-24 °C

Setting the right lighting

Like temperature, lighting requirement varies from species to species and from one stage of growth to another. However, regardless of the species, the following are ideal lighting settings:

- Incubation period – total darkness
- Pinhead formation period – indirect sunlight (or similar illumination from artificial lighting)
- Cropping period - indirect sunlight (or similar illumination from artificial lighting)

Setting the right humidity

Humidity is extremely important. The right humidity will ensure faster growth and optimal production.

The following is the humidity range for the various stages of growth

- Incubation period – 97-100 %
- Pinhead formation period – 97-100 %
- Cropping period - 90 – 95 %

INOCULATE YOUR SUBSTRATE

Inoculating the substrate means to insert the spores into the base substrate (primary substrate).

To inoculate:

1. Create holes into the substrate where you will inject the spores
2. Sterilize the syringe using 99% isopropyl alcohol and dry it
3. Pull the syringe plunger to suck in the spores solution
4. Insert the syringe in one of the holes created and push the plunger to release the spores to release 0.25cc in the hole. Repeat the same for the remaining holes. Make sure that you wipe the syringe using a sterilized cotton swab each time before you make a new injection.

Clean and sterilize the syringe each time you are about to suck in more solutions.

COLONIZE THE TERRITORY

To colonize the territory is to allow the mycelium to spread throughout the substrate or at least occupy most of it.

The colonization process takes about 3-4 weeks. This is after 7-14 days taken for the mycelium to start appearing (germinate).

During colonization, all you need is to monitor the conditions to ensure that there is the right temperature, humidity, and lighting. With the right conditions, the mycelium will colonize the entire territory – that is, if the spores were fairly distributed.

The period by which colonization takes place is called the incubation period. During this period, the substrate is placed in a dark place. It rests undisturbed.

TEND TO THE GROWTH

We have already seen how to set the right condition for the various stages of the shrooms' growth. What is important is to match the right conditions with various growth stages. In this regard, you need to know the expected duration of the various growth periods.

Expected duration for the various growth periods

The duration of each growth period plus the overall growth period depends on the species and the growth conditions. Regardless of the species, growth conditions such as humidity, temperature, and light can greatly alter the duration of each growth stage and the overall growth duration. This is why it is important to ensure optimal growth conditions.

The following is a guideline of the average duration for the various stages of growth:

- Incubation period – 2-4 weeks
- Pinhead formation period – 5-10 days
- Cropping period - 3-7 days

You can see there is a wide range of days for each period. You don't need to worry about whether you are accurate with the incubation period or not. When pinheads start forming, simply know that the incubation period is over.

The cropping period will be ushered in when the pinheads start transforming into caps. Cropping period is the period it takes for the fruit to form and mature. That is, from the beginning of capping to the time of harvesting.

NURTURE THE FRUITS

During the cropping period, the fruit will be formed. During this period, the most important condition that you must observe is humidity. The fruit is over 80% moisture. Thus, humidity is needed for the fruit to be fleshy, puffy, and healthy.

Humidity is achieved through spraying water in the air around the fruit. At this stage, you should not water the substrate.

Temperature is also of critical importance. The abnormal temperature will stunt the fruit. The temperature should be right.

III

HOW TO HARVEST, TREAT AND STORE YOUR PSILOCYBIN MUSHROOMS

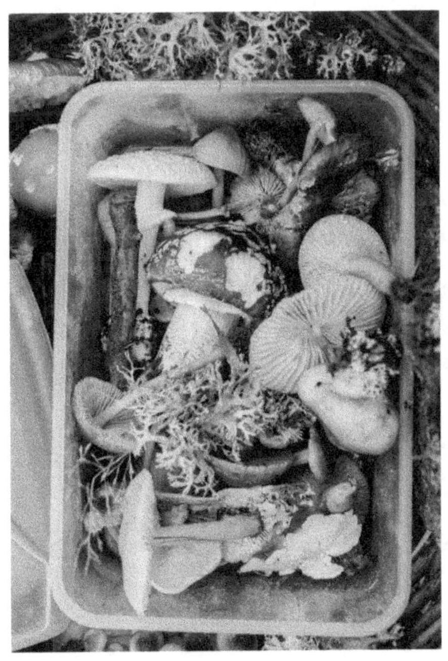

Harvested mushrooms

OVERVIEW

Harvesting mushrooms is not a hard task. However, it needs delicate handling to ensure that you do not destroy the mycelium.

Treating and storing the harvested mushroom is also an easy affair. Just like harvesting, it is also not a hard task. What it requires is extra care to make sure that the potency does not inadvertently diminish due to mishandling or poor storage.

In this Part, you are going to learn the simple harvesting techniques plus basic treatment and storage methods that will ensure that you enjoy the magic potency for days, weeks, and even months to come.

TOPICS COVERED

- How to harvest your psilocybin mushrooms
- How to cure and store your psilocybin mushrooms

7

HOW TO HARVEST YOUR PSILOCYBIN MUSHROOMS

Mushrooms harvested into a basket

Photo by Carboxaldehyde / pexels.com

The moment has now arrived when your mushroom is ready to reward you for your dedicated, delicate, and tireless effort of tending to them. They are now ready to drive you nuts... and skyrocket you to the cosmos of a new reality.

Yet, you want to continue reaping more from every joule of your energy invested in growing these shrooms plus the money invested in buying the grow-kit. The first yield will give you dividends. But as a shrewd investor, you want to continue earning beyond the dividends. You want to earn a bonus from every other cycle you harvest from the grow-kit after the dividends.

To make sure that you earn handsome dividends plus fatty bonuses, I am going to show you how to harvest psilocybin dividends while gaining more from the magical bonuses.

THE TIMING

Not all mushrooms will be ready for picking at the same time. Just as some humans excel in sprinting while others excel in the marathon, some mushrooms will grow faster than others. As a rule of thumb, start harvesting when about three-quarters of your mushrooms are ready.

How do you tell that your mushrooms are ready for harvesting?

For beginners who have not been used to either growing or harvesting mushrooms, it may be quite difficult to tell that their mushrooms are ready for harvesting. Harvesting mushrooms prematurely means that the potency level is not optimized. Harvesting them very late means that there are risks of rotting. You wouldn't like that taste from biting a rotten mushroom.

The following are telling signs that your mushrooms are ready for harvesting:

- **The cap shape:** For most mushroom species, ready mushrooms caps start turning from convex to concave. That is, from turning down to turning up.
- **The veil break**: for those mushrooms that have a veil cover over the gills, watch out for the time the veil begins to break to expose the gills. This signals that the mushrooms are mature and ready for reproduction. By the time the spores start getting released, the more the delay, the lower the potency gets.
- **The spores release**: If you have been late to watch the veil break, or your species require you to just wait slightly after the veil break, watch out for the spores falling. When the spores start to fall, harvest immediately.
- **The darkening edges**: when some mushrooms get mature, the cap edges start darkening. For most mushrooms, the gills start darkening – signaling that spores are mature.
- **The hardening or drying out**: the cap of some species starts hardening or drying out at the edges. The hardening may be accompanied by dryness of the thin cover over the

cap or even cracking of this thin cover. However, the hardening or drying out should be the last sign if other signs haven't manifest. This is because, the hardening, and especially drying out manifest over-maturity. Over-maturity means that you are quite late in your harvest.

Why harvest just before the veil breaks?

For maximum potency, harvest your magic mushroom immediately before the veil breaks from the cap or stem. The veil breaks about 5-12 days after the first pins begin to pop-up. The range is quite wide because, apart from variation in species and strains, variations in environmental factors such as temperature, humidity, aeration, and nutrition can affect this period.

If you intend to flush your grow-kit – that is, reuse it for several cycles of growth after the first harvest, then, you must not allow the veil to break.

When the veil breaks and the spores start falling on the substrate, this triggers the mycelium to release a hormone that allows it to stop the fruiting process and start the colonization process. The consequence is that the grow-kit will unlikely produce further flushes when the colonization process begins.

Again, the released spores will taint and darken the still growing mushroom underneath, thus making them aesthetically less appealing to consume or sell.

THE PICKING

Now that you are sure that your mushrooms are mature, the next thing is to pick them. I assume that you are picking them from the grow-kit. However, the procedure is the same, even without a grow-kit.

The tools

- Surgeon's hand gloves – for making sure that the substrate is not contaminated during harvesting. Make sure that your hands are cleaned, dried, and sanitized before putting on gloves
- Tweezers – for small shrooms that your fingers can hardly reach
- Small brush – for wiping the substrate off the base of the shroom once pulled out
- Container – for putting in harvested mushrooms

Materials

- Gloves – to cover the hands
- Sterilizer – to sterilize the hands and the harvest container

The picking method

Use Twist-and-Pull technique

Procedure

1. Plunge your index finger or thumb to the base of the stem
2. Gently twist and pull the stem until it starts loosening from the substrate. Gradually apply more pull force in case the stem is not pulling up after loosening. Take care not to apply excessive force as this may end up harming the mycelium, thus making it difficult to optimize yield from further flushes. Use small tweezers to pick up smaller mushrooms that may be hard to handle with your hands
3. Use a small brush to gently wipe off loose substrate matter that may cling to the base of the pulled-up mushroom.
4. Repeat the process for other mushrooms till you can harvest all mushrooms.

Once you are done with harvesting your shrooms, the next thing is to store them in such a way that optimizes the potency while rewarding you with extra benefits.

8

HOW TO CURE AND STORE YOUR PSILOCYBIN MUSHROOMS

picked mushrooms

Photo by Albarubescens / CC BY-SA 4.0

You can consume your magic mushrooms while still fresh. You can extend the shelf-life of this freshness by three days. You can achieve this through refrigeration. However, every extra day of refrigeration erodes the shroom's potency – not forgetting the increased risk of molding, rotting, and contamination.

Thus, if you want to retain potency while stretching your consumable shrooms' shelf-life, the best option is to dry the shrooms. Dried shrooms have the added advantage of higher potency per gram (gross). You will have almost 10 times more potency per gram from dry shrooms compared to a gram of fresh shrooms. This also increases the ease of packaging and portability of your shrooms.

HOW TO DRY MAGIC MUSHROOMS

There are three main ways to dry your shrooms:

- Air-drying
- Sun-drying
- Oven-drying

Air-drying

In air drying, you simply expose your shrooms to a fresh supply of dry air at room temperature. This will take the longest period to dry. However, you can accelerate the drying by slightly increasing the temperature of the circulating air.

Sun-drying

This is the most practiced method of drying during summer, especially in the tropical climate where there is plenty of intense sunshine.

Sun-drying relies on the sun rays to dry the mushroom.

The biggest advantage of sun-drying is that your shrooms get more injection of Vitamin D. Thus, their nutritional value increases.

Oven-drying

In case air-drying and sun-drying are not feasible, especially during winter in the cold climates, then oven-drying becomes the most preferred choice.

To oven-dry:

1. Place the shrooms on a paper towel and set each shroom apart from the other
2. Dry the shrooms for about 5 days or until dry while still spread on the paper towel

HOW TO STORE MAGIC MUSHROOMS

Once your shrooms are cured (or dried), it is time to store them.

Storing fresh mushrooms

Fresh mushrooms can be stored for up to 3 days in a refrigerator. Storing fresh mushrooms for more than three days will significantly reduce their potency. Also, the risk of spoilage goes high.

Storing dry mushrooms

The plastic food container is the cheapest and easiest way to store your dry mushrooms.

Procedure:

1. To ensure that the mushroom does not retain or acquire moisture from the sealed-in air, lay a clean paper towel on the inside bottom and inner sides of the container.
2. Put in your dry mushrooms.
3. Optionally, place another clean paper towel on top of the dry mushrooms.
4. Keep the container in a cool dry place. Preferably, keep the container on a shelf or aerated cupboard.

IV

HOW TO CONSUME YOUR DELICIOUS PSILOCYBIN MUSHROOMS

psychedelic tea time

Overview

The climax of your effort comes in reaping its rewards. You have grown and nurtured your shrooms. You've given them the tender care that they deserve.

It is now time that they give you that tender psychedelic love that you desire. This is the best way they can thank you and appreciate you for your effort. However, they only speak through magic. Thus, as their experienced spokesperson, I take this opportunity to unveil their gratitude – a momentous trip to paradise.

TOPICS COVERED

- Your shroom consumption methods
- How to take a dose of your magic
- How to savor your meal-time with shroom edibles recipes

9

YOUR SHROOM CONSUMPTION METHODS

When it comes to consuming your magic shrooms, be creative enough to boost your enjoyment and thus keep monotony at bay.

Several consumption methods exist that you can employ in the consumption of your shrooms.

FACTORS DETERMINING YOUR CHOICE OF CONSUMPTION

Several factors determine your choice of consumption. The following are several factors;

- **Purpose of consumption** – consuming shrooms for recreational purposes might mean a different way of consuming it as opposed to consuming shrooms for therapeutic purposes. For example, for recreational purposes, eat edibles. However, for medicinal purposes, swallow capsules.

- **Convenience** – convenience in terms of portability will give preference to one way of consumption as opposed to another. Capsules are the most portable form of cannabis consumption compared to other forms.

- **Durability and effectiveness of potency** – some methods of consuming shrooms are more potent than others. For example, taking shroom capsules is more potent than raw ingestion (eating raw).

- **Reactionary time** – if you desire a fast reaction from shrooms, it is preferable to take in capsules. However, if you desire a slower reaction, then, edibles become the preferred option.

HOW TO CONSUME SHROOMS

The following are the common methods of consuming shrooms:

- Raw (direct) ingestion
- Shroom edibles
- Shroom powders
- Shroom capsules
- Shroom extracts

RAW (DIRECT) INGESTION

Eating raw shrooms is a common practice. Those who eat raw do it mostly because it is time-saving. However, eating raw increases your chances of nausea. This is because, despite the magic effect, psilocybes are not tasty. Most psilocybes have a rather bitter and unpleasant taste.

SHROOM EDIBLES

Psilocybin mushrooms are just as edible as other mushrooms, only that they have medicinal properties and a rather bitter taste.

Shroom edibles are common these days. Common edibles include:

- Brews and beverages – tea, coffee, chocolate, etc.
- Crunchy snacks – chocolates, cookies, crackers, popcorns, nut mixes, gummy bears, chews, etc.
- Sweets – lollipops, other sweets, etc.

Read Chapter 11 for a collection of delicious shroom edibles recipes.

SHROOM POWDERS

Shroom powders are easy to make. You simply need to dry your shrooms and then pound them into powder. To pound, put the shrooms into a zip-lockable plastic bag and then start pounding using a pestle. Once they attain the powder form, you can place them into a powder dispenser.

Whenever you want to use the shroom powder, simply sprinkle it on your preferred edible. You can also use the powder to make teas just as you use powdered herbs such as ginger and vanilla.

SHROOM CAPSULES

Shroom capsules are filled with dried shrooms. You can either buy them or make them yourself. All you need to make your shroom capsules is to buy the empty capsule casings from the pharmacy and use a spatula to fill in the measured quantity.

Make sure that the measurement is fairly accurate for the same type of capsules so that you can have a fairly uniform effect.

SHROOM EXTRACTS

Psilocybin (or even psilocin) can be extracted from shrooms. This is by far the most concentrated form of shroom magic. These extracts get consumed as sublingual. However, shroom extracts are not so common as edibles and capsules. This is mainly because of the rather long process involved in deriving the extracts.

Shroom extracts are often used as sublingual. Sublingual refers to entry into the bloodstream via the mouth blood vessels, more so, under the tongue. Psilocin can easily be absorbed by mouth's blood vessels. Common forms of shroom consumption through sublingual include:

- The Magic Tinctures

- The Crystals of God

The Magic Tinctures (Holy Waters)

Tinctures are a liquid form of psilocybin extracts obtained through alcohol-based extraction. As such, they contain a small volume of alcohol in them.

How to make magic tinctures

Tools required:

- Small desk fan
- Dust pollen masks
- Bottles with tight caps
- Filter funnel
- Drinking glass
- 10cc syringe

Material used:

- Dried shrooms
- 200 proof ethyl alcohol

Procedure:

1. Cool-dry the mushrooms using a desiccant. Let them be ready for pulverization.

2. Pour the dried mushrooms in a zip-locked plastic bag and pound them with a pestle to pulverize

3. Pour the pulverized mushrooms into a bottle. Tighten the leak-proof bottle-top to seal

4. Pour in the bottle the 200 proof ethyl alcohol till the mixture becomes slurry

5. Stir the content by shaking the bottle. Let the content settle for 24 hours. Afterward, shake it often so that the psilocybin can get off the dry matter and dissolve into the alcohol

6. After another 24 hours frequent shaking, use the filter funnel to isolate the alcohol

7. Pour the remaining slurry into the cloth filter and squeeze it to extract more alcohol into the drinking glass

8. Keep the extracted alcohol into another bottle

9. Soak the extracted shroom material from the filter in more alcohol and repeat steps (5) to (8) for more rounds of filtration

10. Put together all the extracted alcohol into a glass

11. Instigate faster evaporation by using the fan to blow over the glass. You can even use a clean hairdryer to provide hot air that can quicken the evaporation rate.

12. Continue evaporating the alcohol until you attain the required concentration. As a rule of thumb, 1g of dried mushroom should produce 1cc of tincture or less. If 3g can produce 1cc, then that will be a much higher concentration. However, this depends on the potency of the dried shrooms.

13. Store the tincture into a screw-cap bottle and keep it in the freezer.

14. Use the syringe to dispense the tincture. The syringe is ideal because of the more accurate calibration.

The Crystals of God

Crystals of God refers to the powdery crystals of psilocin obtained through the evaporation and crystallization process. Due to their solid form, the Crystals of God lasts longer than the 'Holy Waters'.

The Crystals of God are, in essence, dried Tears of God. Thus, to create these crystals, you build upon the tincture process above.

The crystallization procedure:

1. Pour some few drops of hydrochloric acid into the tincture to achieve a pH level of 3.0

2. Evaporate the acidic content to one-tenth its volume

3. Add paint thinner, cigarette lighter or other nonpolar solvent and gently mix

4. Set the solution for some few hours

5. Free the solution and then pour out the liquid solvent. Alternatively, use the syringe to suck off the floating layer of the solvent after the solution has settled and the layers formed.

6. Gradually add acetone to what is left to remove the remaining solvent. To achieve this, an extra layer will form once the solution with acetone settles. The lower layer will be darker, while the upper layer will be yellowish-greenish.

7. Suck off the top layer using the syringe.

8. Add more acetone. Gently mix, let it settle for some minutes,

and remove the acetone layer by sucking it off using the syringe. A dark, sticky residue will be left.

9. Collect the dark sticky residue into a flatter based wide container just to form a thin layer and let it dry. The thin layer is required to facilitate rapid evaporation. Crystals will start forming.

10. Weigh the crystals to determine their potency.

Note: The thickness of the dark layer will determine the evaporation rate and the size of the crystals. The slower the evaporation rate, the bigger the crystals will be.

Now, the crystals of God are ready for consumption.

10

HOW TO TAKE A DOSE OF YOUR MAGIC

Psilocybin is a powerful drug. Thus, like other drugs, you not only need to ensure that you take the right dosage but also take it responsibly.

While the same dosage may have a different impact on different people, there is a universal dosage scale that anyone can safely use before gaining experience of what works for him/her.

THE DOSING SCALE

It is hard to have a precise dosing scale since the magic potency varies from species to species. Furthermore, the effect of this potency varies from individual to individual, depending on one's body metabolism and experience.

Dry scale

Nonetheless, the following is a dosage scale for dried stems and powder. The scale is derived based on the intended outcome:

- Party dose: 2–3g
- Creative dose: 0.5–1g
- Micro-dose: 0.15–0.3g

Fresh scale

As a rule of thumb, a dry scale is just a tenth of a fresh scale. Thus, for every dry dose, multiply by 10 to get an equivalent fresh dose.

Thus, for fresh consumption:

- Party dose: 20–30g
- Creative dose: 5–10g
- Micro-dose: 1.5–3g

Apart from this scale that is based on the purpose and the intent of consumption, we can also classify the dosage based on whether it is light, medium, or heavy (strong).

Light Dose

Generally, a light dose is about 0.25g to 0.4g. However, this is not a rigid measurement. The most important measure is the effect it generates.

In terms of effect, a light dose is a minimum threshold that brings the user the magic benefits such as mental clarity, mental acuity, and focus but without causing a hallucinogenic effect.

To some users, there will be a light sensation of chill accompanied by the slight vividness of colors. Some users may experience a starry vision while others may experience a unique 'mushroom aura'.

Medium Dose

A medium dose range is between 1.0g and 2.5g. However, like all mushroom doses, the effect varies. Thus, this is just but a rule of thumb. With experience, you will be able to establish your medium-dose based on your experience.

The effects will be a better guide. For a medium dose, you will experience physical symptoms such as dilation of the pupils, dream-like images, and open-eyed visuals.

For most psilonauts, a medium dose opens up the mind to philosophical thoughts and a sense of enlightenment. This can be accompanied by wavy mood swings between euphoria (peak) and dysphoria (trough). The emotional connection also gets augmented.

Heavy Dose

A heavy dose is for experienced heavy-lifters. In this scenario, you are not riding a motorbike as in the light dose, nor a sports car as in the medium dose, but a heavy truck.

In the heavy dose, you carry the full force of the mushroom. It is a full dose. Here, the creative momentum is in full gear.

A heavy dose ranges between 2.0g and 3.5g. Like an experienced truck driver, you must have endurance muscle to navigate the tough terrain that is your trip. The field is wide open, and it is upon you to craft your path.

In the heavy dose, every experience is put to the limit – both positive and negative. If you have a chance for a positive experience, it will be a great positive experience. But, in the unfortunate event that you have a negative experience, it can be a hellish experience.

To mitigate the potential risks of a bad trip, it is important to take adequate preparation. Cultivate your mind for positivity through mindfulness meditation, Neuro-Linguistic Programming, Positive Affirmation, and even Creative visualization. Your state of mind before taking the heavy dose, has a great influence on the kind of trip you will encounter – be it dreams or nightmares.

Physically, if you are not experienced enough, you will need to prepare for negative reactions such as strong nausea. You will probably need some eyeshades just to cover up your inflated pupil from prying eyes. You must also prepare yourself for shocks of the rapid and jarring effects at the start of your trip before the trip smoothens out.

Thus, if you are a beginner, stay away from the heavy lifting. Start light and get accustomed to it before switching to the medium gear.

Furthermore, when you venture into heavy lifting, whether experienced or not, it is important to have a trip-sitter with you. You also need to be in a more familiar environment or an environment adequately prepared for the psychedelic trip, such as psychedelic retreat sites. Also, don't forget to carry your First-Aid kit – just in case you encounter a bad trip that turns awry.

Whichever the dose – whether be it light, medium, or heavy, take it responsibly to mitigate the risk of negative experiences.

HOW TO RESPONSIBLY FUEL YOUR TRIP TO PARADISE

We have already seen that the same level of a dose can have a different effect on different people. Thus, for a beginner, you can never assume that a given dose will not have serious psychoactive effects. So, it is important to always prepare yourself for the trip. Even the most experienced trip-goer does preparation – only more efficiently.

PRE-TRIP RESPONSIBILITY

Like an astronaut preparing for the space mission, you have to exhibit the very same thoroughness as a psilonaut. You are responsible for your mission. Thus, you must take pre-trip responsibility seriously as it is the one that will determine whether you will successfully reach your intended destination or not.

You have to take the following pre-trip actions:

1. *Cast your trip in the mind*

We have also seen that the greatest preparation starts in the mind – like every other journey. Thus, you must set your mind right. A right mindset will more likely map out a more scenic trip. The map work is done in your mind. In this regard, we've seen the importance of mindfulness, meditation, and creative visualization. Practice them in advance, more so when this is your first trip outside the normal reality.

2. Make sure that you are qualified for the trip

The first and foremost thing is to note that the psychedelic trip is for ADULTS ONLY. Thus, if you are below 21 years of age, please, don't board the psychedelic vessel. The legal age of adulthood is 18 years for most jurisdictions. But the legal age is not the same as biological age as some people mature earlier or later than others. 21 years is a sure age in terms of biological maturity.

Apart from being biologically mature, you need to be an ADULT OF SOUND MIND. If you are a mentally unstable person, don't board the psychedelic spacecraft. Furthermore, if you are a trip-sitter, don't do sitting for someone who is not of sound mind, you will bear full blame for the consequences.

While being mentally fit is paramount, there is an exception for certain mental disorders that have been proven to be healed by psilocybin. However, in this case, you need the help of a qualified medical practitioner.

Physical fitness is also important. You are a psilonaut. Thus, don't board the spacecraft to paradise if you have serious infection or disease. Heal first, unless it is a disease that has been proven to be remedied by psilocybin.

3. Have a trip-sitter ready to co-pilot you

Don't go on the trip alone. Have someone sober to co-pilot just in case you lose control of the spacecraft. You need someone to help you read the map, navigate the path, and ensure that you are safely destined.

The person you choose to be your trip-sitter should be someone you trust and is interested in your welfare. Furthermore, the person should be an experienced tripper.

4. *Have the right food and drinks on your trip*

You never know how long your trip could take. You never know how pangs of hunger would behave. As we suggested, the best way to have an impactful trip is to start it on an empty stomach. We also suggested that the trip can take up to 8 hours while in space. You are not on a fasting mission unless you have deliberately decided on that purpose. Thus, while on the trip, you will need to quench your thirst, hydrate your body, and nourish your gut. However, it is a bit challenging when it comes to food. Most psilonaut would rather not eat while on the trip. This is because eating can trigger or aggravate nauseatic sensations. The increased sensitivity of the gut as a result of psilocybin makes your gut more likely to reject certain types of foods.

Apart from having plenty of clean drinking water, you also need to have energizing food. This is to keep you strong and stable as the spacecraft's motion can take you off-balance.

You can also have some sugar-containing drinks for quick effect just in case you experience acute fatigue. However, sugar-containing drinks can shorten your trip. Anyway, a shorter trip is good if you are a beginner.

5. *Keep your environment safe, secure, and serene*

Avoid a cluttered environment. Keep off from hazards such as running machines, flammable substances, a toxic substance, slippery surface, insecure heights, and such others.

To experience serenity, switch off your communication gadgets. This is not the time to risk receiving the bad news that will make you agitated or even good news that will make you overly excited. Also, make sure that in the next 24 hours from the moment you begin the trip is free from important or official appointments.

Avoid taking a trip to crowded places or places with lots of strangers. Strangers may be offended by your weird conduct and become aggressive. Others may seek to take advantage of your condition in case you are out of control, and you have no reliable trip-sitter. As such, avoid tripping while partying in festivals or carnivals.

6. *Keep off other drugs*

Those who are used to taking LSD and mixing this intake with other drugs such as cannabis, tobacco, and alcohol would be more inclined to extend the same to their psilocybin trip. However, the experience may not be the same. It could make matters worse. Your spacecraft could easily go off-path and land you in hell instead of your deserved paradise.

Avoid combining psilocybin with other drugs. Psilocybin likes monopolizing your experience and is extremely jealous of unnecessary competition.

PRO-TRIP RESPONSIBILITY

While on the trip, even though your shuttle is on auto-mode, there are things that you can still be able to do.

The following are actions that you have to take as part of your pro-trip responsibility:

1. *Drink plenty of water*

As a consequence of your body's reaction to psilocybin, you are more likely to dehydrate if you don't drink plenty of water. Already, you took the shroom on an empty stomach, thus, dehydration is the one thing you cannot afford on your trip.

Before your body becomes tolerant of psilocybin, it treats it as a toxin. This is why it uses plenty of water to flush off this 'toxin' from your body.

One fallacy that some have is the belief that drinking plenty of water will dilute the psychedelic experience. This is not the case. Even by drinking plenty of water, you will still experience the same kind of potency. Furthermore, your brain requires to be hydrated to function well. Dehydration can be counterproductive to your intended brain prowess.

2. *Keep off the temptation to become tipsy while on the trip*

Those who are accustomed to drinking alcohol, especially after consuming marijuana, would more likely be tempted to take alcohol while on the psychedelic trip.

The magical effect of the psilocybin mushroom is to accelerate switch over from one thought to another. This high-speed acceleration is what makes the trip enjoyable. However, when you take alcohol while on the trip, it decelerates rather than accelerating your thought-transformation speed. You may start experiencing a sluggish looping of the same thought. This brings a bad experience.

Alcohol is a depressant. It depresses your thoughts and moods. It is the antithesis of psilocybin. So, no need to take it.

3. *Take comfort in the journey*

Once psilocin seizes you and once the shuttle has triggered, you are on auto-mode. Take comfort in your experience by relaxing your nerves and just exploring the scenic visions as they unveil within. Just enjoy the heaven as it clears the fog and opens up the clouds.

Some scenes may be scary along the journey. Don't freak out. Don't let fear bring hell. And some scenes may be profoundly magnificent, don't try to cling to them just enjoy and pass - for more awaits you.

Free your nerves in order to experience the total joy that comes with mental freedom. There is simply no greater freedom than the freedom of your mind. Seize the moment and enjoy it to the fullest.

4. *Take care of your social needs*

Social needs during the trip depend so much on your personality type. For example, most introverts would desire more privacy during the trip and thus would tend to stay alone. On the other hand, most extroverts would desire much closer companionship. However, in certain instances, some introverts become more extroverted, while some extroverts become more introverted.

If you are on your first trip, you may not be able to determine your social needs in advance. But, after several trips, you will be able to tell whether you desire companionship during your trip or not. However, as a beginner, it is prudent that you have a trip-sitter. You can also one or two people you trust to come along with you on your trip. If during the first trip you realize that you need no company, not bad – at least you wouldn't have risked encountering the vagaries of undesired loneliness.

While on the trip, it is important that you communicate and also express your social needs. Some people may want to chat with you when you don't feel like – please tell them in a non-offensive way. Others may want more intimacy while you don't even want to be touched – please let them know. You are on this trip to enjoy it, not to tolerate avoidable displeasures.

5. *Flow with the waves*

There will be high tides and low tides. There will be peaks and troughs. Don't try to flatten the picks and fill the troughs. Simply move with the waves. Keep the motion. Go with the momentum. A safe harbor awaits you… in the end.

While it will be a bit hard for you to flatten the peak, there will be a temptation to gobble up more psilocybin to fill the trough. Be warned. Don't attempt to fill the trough. You never know the magic power of the hidden undercurrents. Tides can easily rise so quickly to overwhelm your vessel. Be satisfied with the motion… and you will become an experienced psilosailor the more you stay calm during your psilovoyage.

Dealing with a bad trip

Experienced astronauts know that not all space missions achieve success. Some turn awry. The same happens with psychedelic trips. While most trips get trippers to paradise, some trips can land trippers in hell.

In the unfortunate case of a bad trip, the trip-sitter must take charge to help navigate the trip shuttle to a safe landing.

The following are important things that a trip-sitter must do:

- Keep the focus on the tripper.
- Take the tripper to a quiet and calming environment where the tripper can sit down for calm breathing. Heart racing is common on most bad trips. Slowing down the breath-rate helps to bring back the heartbeat to normalcy.
- Help the tripper see that the bad trip is not a never-ending endeavor. In most cases, the tripper has lost the essence of time, and one minute could seem a whole day. Fear and desperation heighten when the tripper feels that the situation is not ending. This can cause anguish and even physical agitation.
- Encourage the tripper to drink sweet beverages. Sugar helps to bring down the psychedelic effect
- In case the tripper is extremely agitated and cannot calm down, or you feel that you are becoming overwhelmed, or

that the tripper is in danger, please call emergency services for help. This will enable the tripper to get professional medical attention. Explain to emergency attendants the state of the tripper and what triggered that particular state so that they can provide an appropriate remedy.

Post-trip

Now that you are back to the world, subtly supercharged, you can be a witness to what it means to come back from beyond-this-world. Sometimes you can feel like an alien to your old reality. You are transformed, even in the most infinitesimal way. While physically you may appear the same, your mind is no longer the same. You are in a new normal.

What do you do?

It is time to reflect on the trip experience. I hope it was a trip to paradise. I hold it so. It is time to enliven your paradise here on earth. Keep expanding your alien territory through more trip experiences. And if you are a one who loves the company while on the trip, keep recruiting new psilonauts. And if you are a good storyteller, keep people inspired by your trip stories.

You are now more earthed than before. When the self DIED, it meant that you are newly connected with the nature of beings and the nature of things. Be mindful. Spread compassion. Nurture the good that is beyond the self. Your trip was about exploring heaven beyond the self. Spread this heaven here on earth – in joy, in peace, and harmony.

HOW TO ENGAGE YOUR TRIP GEAR

While cruising on your trip to paradise, you can engage various gears along the way – depending on your dose, experience, and circumstances.

If you are a beginner, the dose you take may push you to a certain gear – even unintended one. However, when you are an experienced tripper, you can manipulate the dose to achieve the desired gear.

The following are the 5 major gears that you can engage to boost your speed range:

Gear 1

This is the *focus gear*.

The first gear ushers at a pretty slow speed. This is the best gear for learners. It is also the right gear for those on micro-dosing to increase mental acuity, think convergently, heighten focus and concentration, and boost productivity.

Taking a trip on this gear will expose you to a luminous experience where you start seeing the surrounding ambiance and colors brightening up. The music starts becoming more intense. You also feel a bit high with a more vibrant spirit. You are now able to see your environment in detail and with greater clarity.

Gear 2

This is the *creativity gear*.

On this gear, you move at a slightly higher speed than the first gear. Your mind starts being bombarded with great ideas. You are thinking fast and in more detail. The colors become brighter, and the ambiance warmer. You feel the music not just intense but throbbing inside your body. Closed-eye visuals begin to cast, plus more animated images start popping up. You become psilosophical.

Gear 3

This is the ***ego dissolution gear***.

It is where you find that your Self DIED.

Tripping on this gear dissolves your ego. You are no longer yourself. There is neither yesterday nor tomorrow. Yesterday died, and tomorrow ceased to be born. Today only comes in momentary drips. You are seized by the moment of now. Time has become an illusion. There is no difference between one minute and one hour. They are both illusions.

The visual impact has become intense. Your pupil is both inflated and dilated. You are now beyond the normal reality. Every form looks distorted and unreal. There is mild hallucination. You are in a new world... experiencing a new reality. You are now a psiloangel.

Gear 4

This is the **object deformation gear**.

Tripping on this gear dissolves the form of objects around you. Objects begin to lose their form within your sight. You can even witness a dog deforming into a dry leaf. You can even witness fence posts deforming into an ostrich that starts talking to you.

On this gear, you experience strong hallucinations. There is an absolute loss of realism. There is a complete percepticide. The magicians in the shrooms have taken over your world. You are being bombarded with one miracle after the other. You are now a psiloghost.

Gear 5

This is the ***universal oneness gear***.

You are in perfect union with everything and every being. Boundaries dissolve. The world that you have always known ceased to exist and DIED with the self. Normal sense, common sense, and logic have already departed from you. You have melted into the universe, and there are only one universal being and one universal intelligence. The power of logic control that you previously exercised simply dissipated into the universe. You are now the omnipotent, omniscient, and omnipresent. You are a psilogod.

11

HOW TO SAVOR YOUR MEAL-TIME WITH SHROOM EDIBLES RECIPES

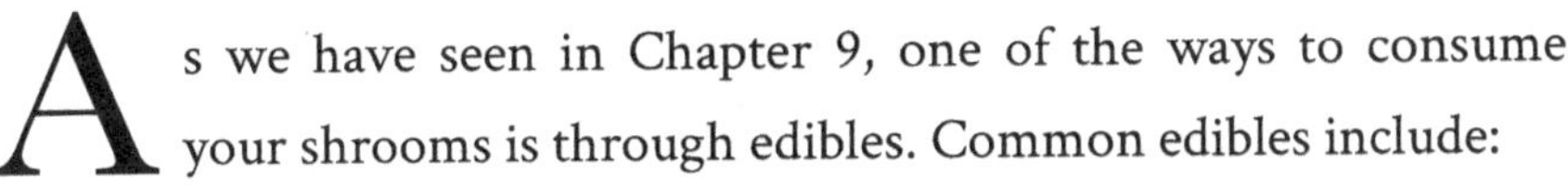

s we have seen in Chapter 9, one of the ways to consume your shrooms is through edibles. Common edibles include:

- Brews and beverages – tea, coffee, chocolate, etc.
- Crunchy snacks – chocolates, cookies, crackers, popcorns, nut mixes, gummy bears, chews, etc.
- Sweets – lollipops, other sweets, etc.

SHROOM BREWS AND BEVERAGES

Brews and beverages are a great way to launch your trip while ensuring that you are sufficiently hydrated. Furthermore, if you are micro-dosing for purposes of work productivity, taking shroom beverages early in the morning as your breakfast can make you have a great mental experience as you work.

Tea is by far the most popular shroom beverage. However, there are many other shroom beverages such as shroom chocolates, shroom juices, shroom smoothies, among others.

How to prepare your psychedelic tea

psychedelic mush tea

Photo by GreenZeb /CC BY-SA 3.0

For tea lovers, psychedelic tea made from shrooms is the best way to jumpstart your day. It is also the best way to neutralize the awful taste of the shrooms on your tongue. Yes, chewing raw shrooms is not an experience that many can cope with. So, tea becomes the savior in this regard.

Dried shroom tea

In the dried shroom tea, you used dried shrooms, either chopped or powdered (or both).

Utensils

Whichever kind of tea you will need to make, the following are basic utensils that you will need

- Teapot
- Kettle
- Mug
- Strainer
- spoons

Ingredients

Basic ingredients:

- dried and chopped shrooms (Shroom powder is preferred)
- Tea leaves (tea bags preferred)
- Boiled water

Optional ingredients:

- sugar
- Honey
- Orange juice (lemon or citrus can also do)

Preparation

1. Pour water into the kettle and heat to the boiling point

2. Put your preferred dose of shrooms powder (or dried and chopped shrooms) into the teapot

3. Pour the boiling water into the shroomed teapot and let settle for a quarter an hour while stirring occasionally and gently

4. Strain into cups, add optional ingredients to your taste and serve

Note: The dosage varies per your needs. For a light dose, you can have 1 gram of shroom powder per cup. For a heavy dose, you can have 5 grams of shroom powder per cup. If you are a beginner, start with the light dose, especially if you are going to add citric fruit juice (citrus, lemon, or orange)

Fresh shroom tea

For preparing fresh shroom tea, utensils and procedures are the same. The only difference is that you are using fresh chopped shrooms as opposed to dry shrooms.

When it comes to fresh shrooms, use about 10 times more quantity of shrooms as you would do for dry shrooms. If you were to use 1g of dry shrooms, use 10gms of fresh shrooms.

Reaping the bonus from your tea

Yes, the first round of tea gives you the dividends for your psychedelic investment. However, it doesn't stop there. If you used chopped mushrooms, then, there is a lot more psilocybin trapped in there after straining. There will still be some traps in the powder, but much less.

So, with chopped shrooms, take advantage of the bonus.

Just put all the shroom residues from the first round into the teapot and repeat steps (1), (2), and (4) above.

The bonus round may not be as potent as the dividend round. Thus, to keep the same level of potency, you may opt to add about one-quarter of the initial dose to the residue to up the potency. Make sure that this addition is a fine powder so that it able to release almost all its potency into the teapot.

Note: If you desire a second round, it is preferable to use chopped shrooms rather than powdered shrooms in the first round. The advantage is that there will be more potency in the residue of the chopped shrooms. This potency will be released quicker into the teapot during the second round than in the first round. Thus, if you desire a second round in quicker succession, this is the way to go.

Truffle Tea

In preparing the Truffle tea, you will need the same utensils as in preparing shroom tea. You will also employ the same procedures.

The only difference is that you will replace shrooms with chopped truffles.

Ginger Twist Tea

Ginger Twist Tea includes ginger and orange juice as basic ingredients. Like tea leaves, ginger is a stomach relaxant and thus helps to remedy stomach upsets. It can also help to relieve nausea. Orange is a great remedy for nausea. Taking orange will help you feel less nausea.

You can either prepare ginger twist tea with dried shrooms or fresh shrooms. The utensils used, and the procedure is the same. The only addition is ginger to the ingredients. Add ginger mixed with shrooms or truffles. Freshly grated ginger matches well with fresh chopped shrooms/truffles. Powdered ginger matches well with powdered shrooms.

In case you are prone to or more susceptible to nausea, use dry powdered ginger instead of fresh ginger.

How to prepare your psychedelic chocolate drink

Chocolate is a rich drink. It not only has great nutritional value but also anti-oxidants that helps to keep premature aging at bay. Thus, combining chocolate with shrooms not only keeps you healthier and happier but also younger.

Utensils

- Teapot
- Kettle
- Mug
- Strainer
- spoons

Ingredients

Basic ingredients:

- shroom powder
- chocolate powder

- Boiled water
- Sugar/honey (optional)

Preparation

1. Pour water into the kettle and heat to the boiling point
2. Put your preferred dose of shrooms powder into the teapot
3. Pour the boiling water into the shroomed teapot and let settle for a quarter an hour while stirring occasionally and gently
4. Strain into cups
5. Add chocolate and sugar to your taste
6. Serve and drink

How to prepare your psychedelic yogurt

If you love yogurt and shrooms, a blend of the two can be a scintillating experience.

Preparation:

1. Put fruit yogurt into a small jug
2. Sprinkle in a measured dose of powdered shrooms
3. Stir aggressively using a whisk
4. Set for about 15 minutes in a refrigerator
5. Serve

Cherry yogurt works best as cherries are great at suppressing the shrooms' awful taste.

How to prepare your psychedelic juice

Fruit juice is extremely refreshing, especially chilled juice during a hot summer season. Adding a dose of psilocybin to the fruit juice can make your drinking sensations more accentuated.

Preparation:

1. Pour your preferred fruit juice into a small jug
2. Sprinkle in a measured dose of powdered shrooms
3. Stir gently and let settle for about 15 minutes while stirring occasionally
4. Use a strainer to sieve the juice into another jug
5. Refrigerate the sieved for about 30 minutes to chill
6. Pour into glasses and serve

How to prepare your favorite lemon elixir

Lemon juice elixir is not only delicious but also relaxing. It works well in toning your gut, thus making you feel a lot more comfortable.

When blending with truffles or shrooms, the cruising speed of your spacecraft not only gets quickly accelerated, but your gut is spared the nauseating resistance to the trip.

Preparation:

1. Chop the shrooms or truffles into small pieces

2. Pour the chops into a mug and squeeze in the lemon juice

3. Set the mug content for 15 minutes, occasionally stirring it.

4. Pour in some sterilized or boiled but cooled drinking water and set for a further 15 minutes, occasionally stirring it

5. Enjoy your elixir

The benefit of shroom tea over chewing the dry shrooms

The following are the key benefits of shroom tea over chewing the dry shrooms:

1. While chewing dry shrooms will start you at normal acceleration, shroom tea starts you at much higher acceleration. Thus, you achieve optimal speed much faster with shroom tea than the chewable.

2. If you intend to switch gears from gear 1 to say gear 2 and then 3 in quick succession, then shroom tea will smoothly switch you over.

3. Shroom tea neutralizes the awful taste of psilocybin in the shrooms. This decreases the degree of nausea.

4. Tea leaves are naturally gut relaxants. Thus, when you add tea leaves to your shrooms, you mitigate the potential effects of stomach upsets. Unless your gut is hypersensitive to psilocybin, you will be able to avoid stomach upsets altogether.

5. There will be quicker absorption of shroom tea as opposed to chewed substance that will need laborious digestion. This absorption can be greatly accelerated by adding citric fruit

juice to your tea. The longer the digestion takes place, the higher is the risk of stomach upsets and nausea.

The benefit of citric fruit juice in your shroom beverages

Adding citrus fruit juice such as lemon or orange facilitates the conversion of psilocybin into psilocin right in the teacup rather than waiting for this to happen in the gut. Thus, the trip receives a big acceleration boost right from the sip. However, the trip lasts shorter than the normal case. You also need to be cautious since the sudden acceleration may push you off-guard. Be prepared for this.

SHROOM SMOOTHIES

Smoothies have a great way of smoothening your alimentary canal and soothing your gut. If you love drinking smoothies, then, you can still enjoy shroom smoothies as part of your psychedelic trip.

Apple-Berry shroom smoothie and Banana-chocolate smoothie are some of the most loved smoothies by psilonaut. This is because of the effect their ingredients have on the gut, especially when it comes to mitigating the effects of nausea.

Apple-Berry Shroom Smoothie

Ingredients:

- ½ glass strawberries (frozen)
- 1 glass raspberry sherbert
- 1 glass apple juice

- 1 ½ glasses lemonade
- Double dose powder of magic shrooms

Preparation

1. Pour all your fluid ingredients into a blender
2. Add the frozen strawberries
3. Pulse-blend the ingredients for 45 seconds
4. Switch the blender's power button to medium range and blend further until the mixture becomes flawlessly smooth
5. Sprinkle in the magic powder and blend further for about 30 seconds just to mix

Banana-Chocolate smoothie

Ingredients:

- 1 glass almond milk (unsweetened)
- 2 pitted dates
- 1 frozen ripe banana
- 1 fresh ripe banana
- 1 teaspoon of protein powder (your favorite)
- 1 ½ tablespoon cacao powder
- 1 dose of magic shroom powder

Preparation:

1. pour all the ingredients into the blender
2. blend until flawlessly smooth

3. pour the smoothie into a glass and serve

CRUNCHY SHROOM SNACKS

Love crunchy snacks? Well, you can also crunch your shrooms as part of your snacks. Shrooms are naturally soft, even when dried. So, to make them crunchy, include them as ingredients in your favorite crunchy snack.

Chocolate is a great ingredient for crunchies, especially chocolate bars. As we have said earlier, it becomes even more important when it comes to conditioning the gut to be more receptive to psilocybin.

I have provided for you Chocolate trip recipe, chocolate truffle recipe, and energy balls recipe to open up your creative mind to more creative recipes.

Chocolate trip recipe

Equipment:

- Microwave oven
- Cooking mold (dinosaur mold is ideal)
- Bowl (for melting the chocolate and mixing it with the shroom powder)

Ingredients:

- Milk chocolate bar
- A dose of magic shroom powder

Preparation:

1. Melt a sizeable portion of the chocolate bar in the oven
2. Gradually sprinkle the magic powder into the melted chocolate while gently stirring
3. Once uniformly stirred, allow it to settle and cool. Make sure that the chocolate doesn't solidify
4. Pour the viscous chocolate onto the mold
5. Place the mold in the fridge for it to solidify
6. Savor your psychedelic chocolate at your convenience

Chocolate truffles

Equipment:

- Microwave oven
- Cooking mold (dinosaur mold is ideal)
- Bowl (for melting the chocolate and mixing it with the shroom powder)

Ingredients:

- Dark chocolate bar
- Chopped magic truffles

Preparation:

1. Melt a sizeable portion of the chocolate bar in the oven

2. Allow it to settle and cool. Make sure that the chocolate doesn't solidify

3. Add in magic chopped magic truffles and gently mix

4. Pour the mixture onto the mold

5. Place the mold in the fridge for it to solidify

6. Savor your psychedelic chocolate truffles at your convenience

Energy balls

Ingredients

- Finely chopped magic truffles
- Coconut flakes
- Rolled oats
- Ground flax seeds
- Raisins
- Cocoa powder
- Peanut butter
- Cinnamon powder
- Vanilla powder

Preparation:

1. Put all the ingredients in a big bowl

2. Mix the ingredients until uniformly textured

3. Roll balls out of the mixture and place them onto a tray

4. Place the balls into the fridge to harden

5. Serve your energy balls at your convenience.

V

HOW TO MAKE YOUR PSYLOCYBIN MUSHROOMS YOUR ETERNAL LIFESTYLE

ecstasy, joy, and happiness

Photo by Hensz / pixabay.com

Eternity is about having a moment that lives in perpetuity through indelible memories of an everlasting transformation.

In life, just as a beautiful landscape, there are highs and lows, twists, and turns. This is what brings up the beauty of life. Life would be miserable if it were flat and happiness like a plain. Happiness manifests in the highs after rising above the lows.

A psychedelic lifestyle does not erase the lows but simply raises the platform so that you can experience higher-highs.

While the psychedelic shrooms raise your platform, it is up to you to accentuate your high-highs through the right dosage and deliberate mind transformation such that you can actualize the psychedelic ideas and psychedelic dreams that abound when you are in that 'cloud 9' where ecstasy, joy and happiness bubble up your volcanic high-highs.

In this Part, we are going to learn how to take the right dose to keep your lifestyle platform raised and to rewire your brain, reset your mind and reprogram your mindset so that you can actualize your psychedelic ideas and live your psychedelic dreams in a new reality.

TOPICS COVERED

- How to use micro-dosing to inspire your daily experiences
- How to recharge your life, boost your joy, and experience more happiness through psychedelic lifestyle

- How to tap into the psychedelic power of shrooms to reset and reprogram your mindset

12

HOW TO USE MICRO-DOSING TO INSPIRE YOUR DAILY EXPERIENCES

Micro-dosing simply means to take doses in minute quantities so that you able to engage in a light conscious trip – a trip that does not bring forth a new reality but brings forth new experiences in the existing reality.

WHY MICRO-DOSING?

In micro-dosing, the purpose is not to take a trip to heaven but to bring heaven into your daily encounters. It is about adding value to your existing reality – work, focus, and productivity.

The following are some of the aims of micro-dosing:

- To have a safe psychedelic trip as a beginner
- To be in control of your daily activities even as you encounter the euphoric moment

Micro-dosing: focus vs. creativity

Do you want to be more focused, or do you want to be more creative?

Different levels of micro-dosing have a different effect on your mind. Also, this is accentuated by the strain of that you choose to extract your micro-dose. Dosing aside, certain strains tend to bring you an experience of mental acuity, while others tend to bring that experience of mental creativity.

Mental acuity increases your level of detail-acquisition. You can absorb more details from a given subject or object. This detail acquisition is a result of convergent thinking whereby different aspects and perspectives of the same object or subject converge to increase clarity, bring more understanding, and give rise to consensus.

On the other hand, mental creativity increases your ability to generate inspiring ideas. Through mental creativity, you can find different ideas of doing the same thing or different ideas of doing different things. Creativity is about diverging from the norm, from the obvious, and the common. Creativity is the outcome of divergent thinking.

While not scientifically proven, most of those who take psilocybin mushrooms in light micro-doses claim to experience improved mental focus. On the other hand, most of those who take heavier micro-doses claim to experience more creativity.

As a rule of thumb, if you want to experience greater mental acuity (focus), take a light dose. On the other hand, if you want to experience greater mental creativity, take a medium dose. If you want to experience hyper-creativity accompanied by complete euphoria and ecstasy, take a heavy dose. However, each individual has different tolerance levels. Again, each strain has a unique impact. Thus, the best way to establish your boundary between focus and creativity can only come through experimentation. Experiment taking different micro-doses and gauge the effect of each quantity of micro-dose on your brain. While carrying out this experiment, also experiment on the different strains/species and their respective impact on focus and creativity.

Nonetheless, generally, lighter micro-doses tend to improve mental acuity, while heavier micro-doses tend to boost mental creativity.

Micro-dosing: rational vs. emotional

Do you want to boost your rational intelligence (RQ), or do you want to boost your emotional intelligence (EQ)?

Generally, a lighter micro-dose promotes rational intelligence (RQ), while a heavier micro-dose promotes emotional connection (EQ).

RQ (Rational Quotient – a measure of rational intelligence) is best applied in the typical classroom/study/work environment. However, when it comes to real-life experience where social networking/relationship is more important, EQ (Emotional Quotient – a measure of emotional intelligence) becomes of more significant importance.

Thus, take a lighter dose if you want to boost your productivity. But if you want to boost your social relationships, take a heavier dose.

Micro-dosing: Therapeutic vs recreational

Micro-dosing is generally for therapeutic purposes. At best, it is for productivity purposes. Micro-doses are too minute to have a recreational impact. Even though you can get therapeutic benefits from micro-doses, you can also gain more therapeutic benefits from recreational doses.

MICRO-DOSING: TRUFFLES OR MUSHROOMS?

Some prefer to micro-dose on truffles while others prefer to micro-dose on mushrooms. Probably, it is a matter of taste and preferences – for each psilonaut has his/her own flight experience. Nonetheless, when it comes to the general effect, there is hardly any difference between truffles and mushrooms.

However, if you are one who desires to store your potent magic for long, then truffles are not your friend. Mushrooms can retain potency for months while dry. But the same isn't the case with truffles. Most truffles diminish their potency as they dry. Truffles are highly perishable when compared to the mushrooms.

Which Psilocybin strain should I use for Micro-dosing?

When it comes to the choice of psilocybin strain to use, it is a matter of personal taste and preferences. However, certain strains appeal to beginners, while others appeal to experienced psilonauts. For example, Golden Teacher seems to favor beginners. PES Amazonian also does well for beginners. B+ isn't bad either.

As a beginner, Golden Teacher is the preferred way to introduce you to the psychedelic kindergarten. Afterward, you can take baby steps towards other strains and species as you gain more experience through experimentation.

Generally, when it comes to species, the following are the most popular species for micro-dosing:

- Psilocybe cubensis
- Psilocybe azurecens
- Psilocybe cyanescens
- Psilocybe semilanceata
- Panaeolus

Nonetheless, any psilocybe can be used for micro-dosing. What you need to factor is the potency of each species so that you can adjust the dosage measurement accordingly.

FINDING THE RIGHT MICRO-DOSE

As a rule of thumb, when it comes to finding the right micro-dose, start low, and gradually increase your dose. However, this rule is more applicable to experienced users than beginners.

Most beginners find it hard to notice the effect of a micro-dose. Thus, for beginners, it is preferable to start with a full dose to learn what it is to take the magic. Afterward, gradually reduce the dosage as the magic sticks. Continue reducing your dose for so long as there is still a magic effect. The lowest level at which you can still experience the magical impact of your shroom becomes your minimum threshold. If you take the path of starting on a full dose, have a trip-sitter to help you navigate the trip.

MICRO-DOSING SCHEDULE

The body always finds ways to adjust and get accustomed to your consumption. If it can't get accustomed to your new consumption habit, then, it will repel your habit.

Similarly, when you take micro-doses, the body tries to adjust and get accustomed to it. As such, it tries to bring normalcy – an old reality. This normalcy tends to nullify the good effect that you desire to get out of micro-dosing.

Thus, to continue enjoying the hyper-moments, you have to trick the body away from normalizing your consumption. How do you achieve this? The simplest way to do this is to avoid micro-dosing daily.

The best approach is to skip two days after taking your dose. For example, if you take your micro-dose on Monday, skip Tuesday and Wednesday so that you take the next micro-dose on Thursday. Tuesday (or the first skip day) is the observation day – a day you observe the impact of your micro-dose. Wednesday (or the second skip day) is the day you take a break from the dose. During the break day, the body has nearly gone to the level (base level) it was in before you took the micro-dose, and thus no longer feels the need to normalize the dosage. However, due to the effect of neuroplasticity on your brain caused by psilocin, the current base level could be higher than the previous base level. The long-term target is to keep on increasing this base level so that every new moment you get on the trip, you achieve a new high-highs.

Knowing that the psychedelic effect only lasts for 8 hours (time it to match with your working hours for maximum productivity), on the first skip-day, you will simply be riding on the left-over psychedelic waves. The second skip-day will have no noticeable waves to ride on. It is the day of sobriety. It the day of the 'lull before the next storm'.

I would recommend making the pattern very irregular so that the body has no chance of normalization and hence nullifying the psychedelic effect.

HOW TO TAKE YOUR MICRO-DOSE

You can take your micro-dose in several ways. The following are the two most loved ways by psilonauts:

- Capsules – you can either buy ready-made psilocybe capsules, or you can simply pour your measured psilocybe powder into empty capsules, store them into a bottle, and take each capsule as needed.
- Honey beverage – if you like fluid dose, simply sprinkle your micro-dose into a cup of hot water. Add several drops of honey to boost your taste. Stir and then drink as a beverage. The advantage of honey is that it not only suppresses the bitter or unpleasant taste but also boosts the absorption rate of the micro-dose.

13

HOW TO RECHARGE YOUR LIFE, BOOST YOUR JOY, AND EXPERIENCE MORE HAPPINESS THROUGH PSYCHEDELIC LIFESTYLE

You can achieve a psychedelic lifestyle. You can be a constant psychedelic voyager.

You can recharge your life. Nature's secretly hidden recharge battery is now within your reach. All you need is to tap into its endless reserves. In Part II, we discussed how you can keep this battery within your reach and how you can ensure that this battery keeps the high voltage at all times.

The radiance of constant joy in this gloomy world is a rarity. Just as there are those days when the sun rises late and those days when the clouds overwhelm its rays, there are certainly those days when the gloom blankets your radiance. But, despite the gloom and the darkness, the sunshine never switches off. Its source of radiance remains constant. Similarly, I cannot promise you that your joy will shine all moments, but I can promise you that its source will never extinguish, for so long as the magic source remains supplied.

Happiness is not something to be pursued. Rather, happiness is something to be experienced. Just as you expose yourself to early sunrise so that your skin can experience that morning glow and its accompanying soothing warmth, you too can expose yourself to happiness. It takes effort. It is not that happiness doesn't exist. It is simply that very few know how to expose themselves to its rays.

Having a psychedelic lifestyle is the way to recharge your life, boost your joy, and experience more happiness.

SO, WHAT IS THIS PSYCHEDELIC LIFESTYLE?

A psychedelic lifestyle is that lifestyle characterized by a constant trip to nirvana. Like every other long trip, there are moments to take a break and rest. There are moments to re-energize and moments to take a nap. This doesn't mean that the trip has ended, but still ongoing and still transitioning from one stage to another. You are still arriving!

A psychedelic lifestyle is a lifestyle that is constantly being recharged by the magic battery. You are constantly arriving. In this lifestyle, energy and vitality keep flowing from this magic battery into your gut, veins, and nerves. Your brain is constantly being nourished, and your mind constantly recharged.

HOW DO I ACHIEVE THIS PSYCHEDELIC LIFESTYLE?

As I have said earlier, there will be a boom and gloom. And there will be breaks and rests. But, just as the sun never switches off despite the darkness, the psychedelic lifestyle doesn't end with momentary breaks. And like any other flow, there will be ups and downs. Energy is a flow. And this flow has its waves. You may have low-energy moments, and you may have high-energy moments. What would be the need for a magic battery if all moments were high moments?

Thus, achieving a psychedelic lifestyle means keeping your magic battery in constant supply and letting it keep optimal recharge level. Optimal means just sufficiently enough to maximize benefits – neither extremely high nor extremely low – for the extremity of both polarities have costs that supersede the benefits. You want a positive gain, not a negative loss.

Well, how do I keep on recharging?

There are six things that you must do (or rather, six steps that you must take):

1. Be open-minded
2. Set your vision
3. Keep a prepping routine
4. Keep a dosing routine
5. Take charge
6. Have faith

Be open-minded

To be open-minded is to be free to experience what comes by without attachment to a certain specific outcome. This does not necessarily mean that you have no hope for a certain experience. But, even with that hope, you don't set expectations. I hope for something but expect anything. I hope for a certain experience but expect any other outcome.

Why should you be open-minded?

The primary reason is that every psychedelic trip is unique. You can experience heaven – bliss, eternal joy, endless laughter, perma-smile, or perma-grin. Great ideas can flow in quick succession such that you see the philosopher in you sitting on top of the universe and providing all the solutions that the world needs. You too can experience hell – confusion, discomfort, terrifying ghostly images, panic, among others. What you experience is more often the reality mingled with the past mental images.

To be open-minded is to accept infinite possibilities. It is also to accept that any experience is possible. Thus, you set your mind free to experience whatever comes by without attaching your emotions to it.

Being open-minded is to free yourself from conditionalities. It is to stop forging or corrupting your new experience pre-birth with elements of your previous experience.

This may run contrary to my assertion of what you expect on your psychedelic trip. It may even seem to run contrary to my next assertion that you need to set vision/goals. However, this is further from what is.

In the open-mindedness, you are a constant traveler to unknown destinations. You are an adventurer. Though you've heard stories of someplace and what you ought to do to arrive there, and how the path to that destination is plus the experiences of other voyagers, you do not let these fix your destiny. You simply don't know the destination. Their stories and experiences are simply theirs, not yours. You are yet to experience.

Furthermore, in this psychedelic trip, you are not the driver, rather the passenger. You are not engaged in the mechanics that bring forth movement, but simply an observer. You are not crafting the path, but simply experiencing it. You have no control over the program that runs the shroom's spacecraft, but you have control over the program that runs your experience.

Set your vision

As I have said before, oftentimes, your state of mind before the psychedelic trip counts a lot in what you experience along that trip.

When you have more positive mental images than negative ones, you are more likely to experience a heavenly trip. But, if you have entertained a lot of negative mental images before the trip, then, you are more likely to encounter a hellish experience on your trip. Whichever the case, the good thing is that the experience temporary.

Setting your vision helps to flush out negative mental images. But this can only happen if you set up a positive vision.

Creative visualization is one great way to set up a positive vision. Through creative visualization, you can create positive mental images of your trip. Thus, as the psychedelic magic lifts you, the boundary between your reality and vision gets nullified as you slowly dive into your created vision. This way, you can avoid hell on your trip. The creative visions you have becomes the mental maps to your destiny.

Create a mastermind alliance

We exist because of others and for others. This is the reality that we have never fathomed deeply. The ego is a very small part of our existence. It is because of others that you were conceived. And it is because of others that you have learned a lot. And it is for others that you have a job, a profession, a trade, business, or whatever livelihood that you have pursued.

Similarly, your trip, if it got to be successful, depends on others. This is more important when it comes to psychedelic trip. You are a psilonaut. And like astronauts, you need a team for a successful take-off into your space exploration.

Create a mastermind alliance that will make it possible for you to successfully launch your spacecraft into nirvana.

Just as there is a need for a co-pilot, co-driver, etc., you need to have a trip-sitter. A trip-sitter will help you out on your journey.

Keep a prepping routine

Though the psychedelic trip lasts for a few hours, it can be a very long timeless mental journey. Sometimes, a few hours can look like years.

Thus, you have to prepare yourself as you would do when you are going for a very long journey.

However, timelessness is not an experience for everyone. But, if you are new to this trip, you are not sure whether you will fall into timelessness or not. Thus, factor the timelessness into your trip.

HOW DO YOU PREPARE YOURSELF FOR THE LONG TRIP?

The following are some of the ways by which you can be prepared for the long psychedelic trip:

1. *Have the right mindset*

We have already discussed being open-minded. That is the right mindset that you need to cultivate as your mental preparation.

2. *Have the right vision of your destiny*

Setting your vision is part of your preparation for this psychedelic trip. We've seen the importance of creative visualizations in your psychedelic endeavor.

3. *Pack your belongings*

What belongings do you need to have for your trip? Knowing that you are going to take a flight, it simply means that you must travel light – with only essentials. Don't cling – be it physically or mentally, to baggage that can only serve to burden and clutter your trip. Essentials include:

- Plenty of water
- Light food (such as energy drink, citric fruit, etc.)

4. Dress well

Yeah, when going for a long trip, especially as guests of honor, we dress exceptionally well. This is no exception when it comes to psychedelic trip. But don't forget that you are a psilonaut! Thus, there is a special requirement for your dressing.

Have a light, fairly loose dress. Don't wear a very tight dress that limits your flexibility and movement. Also, don't wear a very loose dress that can cause you to stumble. The dress should fit your body well.

Nonetheless, choose the color scheme that brings radiance. A color scheme that helps to set a positive spirit. Fairly bright but uncluttered colors are ideal.

5. Eat well

Eat well! This seems an irony. Why? Because the ideal eating for a light flight is to avoid being heavy. Furthermore, your tummy may not be such receptive to the shrooms. Thus, the safest way is to eat the shrooms on an empty stomach to avoid the clash of shrooms with the food that you've eaten.

But an empty stomach does not mean you eat when hungry. Simply eat some hours early so that by the time you take your trip, what you ate is already digested.

If you can practice Intermittent fasting with an 8-hour fasting window before your trip, that will be great. You can then match the fasting window with your trip. A 10-12 hour fasting window can be much better just to take care of the extremities of the psychedelic trip. With a 10-12 hour fasting window, you can begin the trip an hour or two into the fasting window and therefore end your trip an hour or two within the fasting window. This way, you are not disturbed by the pangs of hunger during your trip.

If you want to take advantage of Intermittent fasting during your trip, practice fasting at least a week before the start of your trips.

Keep a dosing routine

If your life has to remain magically recharged, keep dosing. We've already seen how to micro-dose yourself to stay euphoric.

The dose is the real charge material for your lifestyle battery.

Take charge

Whether you are piloting your spacecraft, or you are a passenger, or the spacecraft is simply on auto-mode, you still need to take charge.

No one else, but you are in charge of your experience. Your experience is unique to you. You may encounter the same circumstance with someone else, go through the same situation with the same person, but you will never have the same experience.

Your experience is not what happens to you but how you react to the happenings. Take charge of your experiences.

Have faith

Faith is not about believing or trusting. It is not about religion. It is simply setting yourself free from worries and expectations. Journeys have their risks. Accidents can occur. But, as a psilonaut, these should not beset you. Your focus is on your destiny and the experiences that come along the way.

Faith is an attitude of mental, psychological, and spiritual freedom. In faith, you loosen out your attachment to expectations. In faith, you can declutter your path from the dirt of limiting beliefs, the vicious cycle of destructive habits, and unfounded fears.

How do I drive into eternity?

The best way to drive yourself into a psychedelic eternity is to practice a psychedelic lifestyle. In the psychedelic lifestyle, you are on an endless psychedelic trip. You are still arriving… and endlessly arriving.

As we have seen, on this endless trip, there are breaks, and rest – just like any other long journey. The most important thing to note is that even when the euphoric moment wanes, there is a long-term transformation of your state of mind. In this transformation, some occurrences are permanent – such as the psychedelic effect of neuroplasticity on your brain. The platform from which you take off rises to a new level with every new launch of your psychedelic shuttle.

For example, some form of neuroplasticity takes place. In this neuroplasticity, your brain gets permanently rewired. Once this rewiring takes place, it is bound to be permanent. Every time you get on the psychedelic trip, this rewiring gets reinforced.

While there is a big difference between being eternal and everlasting, to a certain degree, you can achieve both. Some form of your brain rewiring can be everlasting. Some kind of experience that you gain is eternal. It is not that these experiences are everlasting, but their impact is unforgettable. Eternity is more about being unforgettable than being everlasting.

PSYCHEDELIC RETREAT

One of the best ways to recharge your life and boost your energy level is to go for a psychedelic retreat. Psychedelic retreats are common these days. It is just a retreat-like any other, save for the fact that it is energized by the psilocybin.

Apart from tripping on the magic spacecraft as a psilonaut, you are in the company of fellow psilonauts and professional trip-sitters.

The location for psychedelic retreat is no ordinary site. It is carefully selected for your space launch. All potential hazards are removed. Safety is of utmost importance. First-Aid and emergency assistance are in top-gear.

While you can create your retreat location as you would do with a picnic, it is best to let the professionals do it for you. This is because they have the experience and are prepared to handle any kind of emergency that may arise should the spacecraft wobble or develop some mechanical problems.

EMOTIONAL CONNECTION

Emotions are vital energy waves in our bodies that enable us to communicate through feelings. The most powerful connection between people is an emotional connection. It is the emotional connection that creates the most enduring and lasting bond.

Unfortunately, in our modern lifestyle, emotions are washed away by the demands of our careers, professions, jobs, and etiquettes. We have been trained to mute our emotional expressions to appear 'professional'. Over time, through 'learned non-use', our emotional connectors become dysfunctional, ineffective, and even diminished.

Through the psychedelic trip, we can transcendent the 'petty decencies' of professional demeanor and reach out to one another in a more natural way, bereft of emotional connections, loneliness, and boredom creep in. These two dampens our moods and thus breed depression. Unchecked and unremedied, depression becomes a mental illness that ends up negatively affecting every facet of our life – and even terminate it. This is probably one of the reasons why psilocin has been found to 'miraculously' heal the 'treatment-resistant' depression.

To recharge your life, boost your joy, and experience more happiness in your life, you need to be emotionally connected with people. Get under the umbrella of psilocybin mushrooms, and you could find safety from the dilapidating rays of loneliness.

SOCIAL CONNECTION

We are social beings. As social beings, we can hardly exist without social connections. One of the leading causes of mental disorders is poor social connection. There is clear scientific evidence that there is a correlation between depression and physical disorders such as obesity. To a certain degree, depression can cause obesity. On the other hand, obesity can cause heart problems, diabetes, and other diseases. Thus, whatever increases your social connection boosts not just your mental health but also your physical health and overall health.

Psychedelic mushroom has been found to boost social connections not just among those who consume it but also between the consumers and non-consumers. This is primarily because psilocin is an ego buster. Selfish ego is what creates a wall between people. So, when this selfish ego is dissolved, then, an individual finds no reason what-soever to buttress himself from those others who have no intent to cause harm.

EGO DISSOLUTION (EGO BUSTER)

As Buddha taught, our suffering is caused by our selfish desires. These selfish desires are triggered by a selfish ego. From a psychological perspective, the ego as a whole is not bad. It is out of ego that we can express our individuality and achieve our highest aspirations. However, when this individualism (id) goes against the welfare of others and even our very own welfare, then it becomes destructive.

When ego dissolution is mentioned, it is not about killing the ego as a whole, but getting rid of that selfish individualism.

WHEN THE SELF DIED

Have you ever encountered someone whose self has DIED?

Well, it is frightening to even think about it. However, Drug-Induced-Ego-Dissolution (DIED) is a great thing. Psilocybin is such a powerful drug when it comes to inducing ego dissolution.

When you board the psilocybin spacecraft, your selfish earthly being is left behind. You experience a new mystic angelic world where you see other beings as great beings to embrace in your mind and heart. Your social magnetism becomes more powerful as you seek to bring more people into your field of magnetic excitation.

PSYCHEDELIC MEDITATION

Meditation has been practiced for thousands of years. The same is the case with the consumption of psychedelic mushrooms. The common bond between meditation and psychedelic mushroom consumption is that both of them have been traditionally taken by ancient societies to achieve a desired spiritual state.

Before we can explore more on psychedelic meditation, let's first understand what meditation is, its benefits, and how to practice it.

What is meditation?

Meditation is the process of bringing yourself back to a state of being by which your self-awareness is optimized. When you meditate, you can stop following the maps that have been ingrained into your mindset to enable you to carry out daily routines. In meditation, you can reconnect with your inner being and reflect from within.

Like with those whose self has DIED, meditation detaches your being from the selfish, egoistic attachment to thoughts, concepts, perceptions, attitudes, beliefs, and even habits. You can watch them as they get washed by the gushing river that runs in your mind where such thoughts, concepts, perceptions, attitudes, and beliefs are merely an array of flotsam bubbles.

What if you get into that meditative state after the self has DIED? Unimaginable! Yet, this what means to be under the cover of a psychedelic umbrella.

What is psychedelic meditation?

Psychedelic meditation is the kind of meditation that precedes or is taken in tandem with the psychedelic trip – or even immediately after the psychedelic trip.

The purpose of meditation is to promote a pleasurable yet mindful experience before, during, or after the trip. On-trip psychedelic meditation is ideal when you are on a micro-dose. Otherwise, for a heavy dose, you either meditate before or after the trip. You can also meditate both before and after the heavy trip.

If you are new to the psychedelic world, it would be quite difficult to meditate while on your psychedelic trip. However, the best way to blend these two powerful mind-transforming techniques is to practice each separately till you are excellent in each. Once you become excellent in each, you can then start to gradually take steps to fuse them.

The benefits of psychedelic meditation

Meditation has been found to declutter your mind and thus bring forth clarity and a better perspective. This helps one to make more rational decisions that help to prevent pitfalls that perpetuate the vicious cycle of stress, anxiety, and depression. In this regard, meditation acts as a coolant and pacifier. A coolant in the sense that it cools down the nerves, thus relieving stress. As a pacifier, meditation brings stillness of the mind, just as one would bring stillness of the water in a container to let sediments settle down for clean water to be drawn.

The magic in the shrooms crystalizes this cooling and pacification outcome from meditation and thus anchors the ensuing stillness to the ground. This creates a strong foundation for fortitude. In this regard, the shroom's magic acts as the catalyzing agent that compacts the solidification during the crystallization process.

With a clarity of mind, meditation helps to bring your mind to higher levels of concentration and focus. Higher concentration and focus boosts productivity as you can prevent the dissipation of energy towards unnecessary clutter. When your mind is decluttered, creativity is optimized. As a catalyst, a micro-dose of the magic shrooms intensifies this focus and optimizes productivity.

By relieving stress and depression, meditation helps to prevent or relieve mental conditions that are often triggered or aggravated by these two factors. Thus, meditation is therapeutic. We've also seen the power of magic shrooms as mental therapy. Blending meditation with the magic from shrooms brings up a more powerful dose against stress and depression.

Some of the therapeutic attributes of meditation include boosting immunity, prevention of premature aging, boosting libido, promoting reproductive health, and advancing overall sexuality. Furthermore, meditation helps to relieve pain sensations. The magic shrooms inject a dose of joy and ecstasy to this relief.

The psycho-spiritual aspect of meditation is that it boosts one's spirituality, releases held-up emotional energy, and thus getting rid of anger and grief. In this regard, meditation helps to boost your self-esteem, which results in greater self-acceptance and improved self-confidence. The entheogenic effect of magic shrooms advances this boost - in addition to making your grounded and free from attachments to a negative self-image that breeds fear.

When it comes to physiological health, meditation lowers your breathing rate and, with it, lowers your blood pressure, which is important in preventing or relieving hypertension.

Grounding yourself as a precursor to psychedelic meditation

Grounding yourself simply means putting your mind to rest. Most of the time, your mind is roving randomly like a kite in the air. In this roving process, it fumbles upon different currents of thoughts. And like following the direction of the wind, it flows along the direction of the most powerful thoughts, the most captivating thoughts, or simply the most traditional thoughts. These thoughts aren't necessarily the most transformative or the most creative. They are simply the most influential.

Putting your mind to rest is to bring it to consciousness. To see this roving for what it is. And to halt your mind's movement as an agent of the thought currents.

By grounding yourself, you can experience what is real: the real you that is free from perceptions, sensations, and emotions - A self that is free from cultures, traditions, beliefs, and knowledge.

Naturally, it is rather hard to ground yourself when these currents are still flowing. However, with psychedelic effects from the mushrooms, this settling down, this grounding, becomes magical. Psilocin acts like an agent that helps the various 'particles' of your mind hitherto dissipated by the powerful thought currents to consolidate and thus gain a critical mass to sink to the ground.

Thus, psilocin acts as a catalyst for your grounding, making it easy for you to quickly get grounded.

Meditation: how to get started

Meditation has no straight-cut formula. What is important is that you create that environment for meditation... and, more importantly, create that mindset for meditation.

A meditative mindset is one that is ready to detach. Detach from beliefs, myths, anxieties, worries, expectations, and such other kinds of psychological attachments. Thus, to cultivate that meditative mindset, switch off those mind buttons that complete the circuit to each of these attachments. This is akin to pressing the button to switch off the lighting.

A meditative environment is one that allows serenity to set it. Just as water requires to be still so that sediments settle down, your mind requires stillness for the mind clutters to settle down so that you can enjoy the mind's purity. To achieve this, make sure that your place for meditation is decluttered, clean, silent, and serene. If you are planning to sit or squat, then have a comfortable fabric to sit or squat on, such as carpet or mat.

Once you have set up the right meditative mindset and meditative environment, the next thing is to set up a meditative posture. A meditative posture is simply a posture that avoids physical stress and strain. When you experience physical stress and strain, that will ring in your mind and thus disrupt your meditative mindset. Getting seated in a comfortable posture that you have practiced long enough is the best option. In most oriental societies, sitting with legs crossed is often the best posture. However, you should not compel yourself to do such, if that doesn't make you comfortable.

After gaining the right posture, the next thing is to focus and concentrate. Focusing is a prerequisite to concentration. If you are a beginner, you can focus on a physical object in front of you. Let that object be still. Focusing on a mobile object or a shaking object can disrupt your concentration. You can also focus on the ground ahead or even a wall. What is important is that your point of focus is still uncluttered, and does not strain your posture.

Once you are focused, the next step is to focus your mind inwards. You can do this by observing your heartbeat or breathing rhythm. Gradually lower your pace of breathing while also increasing the depth and duration of your inhalation and exhalation. This serves to reduce your heart rate, lower your body activity/metabolism to the basal level. The main intention is to relax your body so that there is less pressure that causes stress or strain on the brain.

The final stage of this meditation is to switch the mind from being seized by the thought process. Free your mind from the thought pattern by not making a conscious effort to digest what the thought is about.

Continue your focus and concentration until you feel like stopping. When you feel like stopping, don't force yourself to prolong any further – unless you are just training your mind and body for endurance. Letting meditation end naturally just as sleep does is the best way.

If you can arrive at that state when you are no longer consciously aware of your thoughts, then that is the apex point of your meditation. It is like reaching the apex of Mt. Everest.

Make meditation your daily routine so that you perfect it with every new practice session.

Practicing psychedelic mindfulness

Mindfulness brings self-awareness while psilocin brings rootedness. By practicing mindfulness, you can disentangle yourself from the currents of your thought process. You set your mind free to root in the ground - to be anchored, so that chaotic thought currents do not lift you off during your trip.

Mindfulness is important in your trip as it helps you to develop that capacity to isolate the useful reality from phantasmagoria. This ability to distinguish the real experience of the trip from the delusions helps you to remain focused and thus overcome the dangerous currents that would easily seize you and rove you up to hell. Such currents include emotions, fears, anxieties, and worries.

Integrating your reality

Integration is simply about bringing different facets of your reality that had hitherto been forcefully disintegrated by the strong currents of distorted reality. It is the consolidation and crystallization of your pure reality – devoid of the impurities. Such impurities include toxic emotions, destructive thought patterns, rigid attachments, and selfish ego, among others.

In the psychedelic sphere, integration is about merging your trip experience with that experience gain from a mindful state of being grounded and then crafting a new lifestyle out of this merger. This lifestyle becomes a new state of being: a new being that is larger than the total of its constituent parts - A fusion.

In the process of integration, there is no predefined mapwork. The growth of the new being takes its course – just as the birth of a new mushroom. All you can do is to set the right conditions for the growth of this new being. Mindfulness, meditation, and positive experience from trip navigation become the critical ingredients of these right conditions.

Engendering an attitude of openness to new experience, being non-judgmental, and being attentive is the most important attitude to achieving a higher state of integration.

Devoting to your new paradigm of reality

Once you have achieved a state of integration, the next thing is to devote yourself to that new state of reality. You focus your attention on your new altar of self-awareness.

Why devotion? Don't forget that it is the nature of the mind to wander – for so long as thought currents keep flowing. It is also the nature of thought currents to keep flowing. In devotion, you keep your integrated being free from the effects of the flowing thought currents. To stop it from being a mere flotsam object susceptible to the chaotic bombardments of random thoughts.

Having faith in the source of your newly transformed lifestyle, having faith in this transformative agent, and having faith that every other trip will bring forth a new transformative experience is what it means to be devoted.

CULTIVATING A BEGINNER'S MIND

Every psychedelic trip is new and unique. You may be an experienced driver, but that does not necessarily mean that you are experienced in all journeys that you are about to undertake, or you will ever undertake. Similarly, you may be an experienced psilonaut, but that does not mean every trip will be the same.

There is a lot to learn on every trip you make. To be a great psychedelic learner, you have reset your mind afresh. You have to vacate memories of the previous trips from it. You have to empty your mind so that an optimized psychedelic learning can take place.

Cultivating a beginner's mind is to always take every other trip as a fresh opportunity to experience newness. The old experience DIED on the old trip. The old lessons DIED with it too. You cannot vacate your skills as a psilonaut, but you can vacate your experiences. Your knowledge may be adulterated, but your skills are pure. Skills are a product of distilled experience.

Why cultivate a beginner's mind?

We've already seen why it is important to be open-minded. We've also discussed why meditation and mindfulness are important in advancing this open-mindedness.

A beginner's mindset allows tripping through an uncharted path. Without cultivating a beginner's mind, you are more likely to trip through the beaten path. Even though there will be some new experiences along a beaten path, a lot of experience will be stale.

How to engage in psychedelic Learning

In psychedelic learning, you take advantage of the psychedelic trip to veer off the beaten path so that you can create your novel path. You can hardly learn anything new in the beaten path – for all knowledge is the product of the beaten path. Knowledge is stale. Yet, the psychedelic experience is fresh.

Carrying out mindfulness meditation is a way to remove clutters of old knowledge from your mind as you expand the capacity of the emptied space to acquire new lessons. This is probably the reason why creative minds love micro-dosing as they carry out their creative endeavors.

In psychedelic learning, you adopt an attitude of openness. You detach yourself from preconceptions and other people's perspectives. What you learned before becomes immaterial to the new opportunities yet to unveil on the new trip. It is only through this attitude that opportunities for radical breakthroughs are optimized. Open-mindedness affords you the opportunity for deep learning. You don't engage in the routine of scratching the surface of knowledge through repetitions, regurgitations, and memorizations. You simply avoid assuming the posture of knowing and thus take every other trip and every other person you encounter along the trip as a potential teacher – someone with something to teach you.

PSYCHEDELIC RELATIONSHIPS

Magic shrooms not only work their magic on your brain and mind but also work magic on your relationships. Your relationships get enhanced when you are on a psychedelic trip. This is because of the newly built emotional connections that allow recharged energy flows to reconnect with those of others.

From psilonauts own experiences, the following are some of the prosocial behaviors that they observed while on the trip:

- More connectedness
- Fewer ego conflicts
- Less anxiety, stress, and depression that tend to poison relationships
- Greater perspective one's role in the relationship

Psychedelic marriage recipe

An increasing number of marriage therapists are taking advantage of psychedelic retreats to heal marriage divisions and conflicts and thus forge a stronger bond between couples.

The following is a common psychedelic marriage recipe that you can use to create a stronger marriage bond with your partner:

- Set a romantic environment: declutter, dim lights, candle-lit psychedelic dinner,
- Take psychedelic dinner together (including a glass of red wine?)
- Have some few psychedelic bites while in bed.
- Have some psychedelic conversation
- Engage in psychedelic romance
- If set, have psychedelic sexual escapades

HOW TO SHARE YOUR PSYCHEDELIC VISION AND IDEAS WITH THE WORLD

The world happens because of ideas.

A vision is simply that grander picture formed from pixels of ideas.

If the world has to change, then, new ideas and greater vision must come forth.

These ideas and visions do not come from supernatural beings, but human beings like you and me. Unfortunately, there are zillions of ideas that die because they were never shared. Visions turn dark because they were simply left to die stillborn.

We do the world a great disservice if we let our ideas perish and our visions abort. It is time to honor our ideas and enliven our visions.

With a micro-dose of magic shrooms and creative visualization, we can enliven our visions through the following 7 steps:

1. *Dream big*

We all dream. Everyone dreams. Yet, not all dreams are big enough to move the world. This calls for us to dream big.

To dream big is simply to create captivating dreams that can transform us, others, and the world.

It is not that there are only a few of us blessed with the ability to dream big. No. It is that only a few spare enough energies and put enough effort to create, nurture, and give life to their dreams.

Seize the oneirogenic power of psychedelic shrooms to dream big.

2. *Visualize your dream*

Dreams come and go. Unless you visualize them, they won't stick around.

To visualize a dream is to add imagery to it so that not only you but others too can be able to see it as you do, once you share it out.

Not until visualized, a big dream is simply a big idea. Visualizing it gives it a life form of its own. Making it have life means that it is not just a still picture but a motion being. It moves and captivates those who come into encounter with it. It is empowering, stimulating, and transformational. People can see that transformational potential. They can feel it. And can associate with it.

Tap into the power of psychedelic micro-dose to creatively visualize your dream.

3. Cast your dream on a grander form

Once you have visualized your dream, cast it on a grander form. Yes, use words that make it easily understood. Use words that make it highly captivating. Use words that make those you share it with feel that they instantly belong to it.

Tap into the mystic power of magic shrooms to inspire people's emotional connection to your dream.

4. Describe your dream's core elements

The vision is like a forest on the horizon.

People can see how it perfectly covers the landscape. However, they cannot see the trunk, the branches, the leaves, the flowers, and, more importantly, the fruits.

Zoom your perspective so that you bring the forest closer to them in such a way that they can see the individual trees; their spirit can dance with the trembling leaves; their nostrils can partake of the nectar's sweet aroma, and their appetites can be drawn to the ripe fruits beckoning their harvest.

Let the creative power of the mystic shrooms magnify the core elements of your vision.

5. *Package your dream in an appealing wrap*

If you have ever been a marketer or knows what marketing is all about, you cannot ignore the importance of packaging. Well, every grown-up adult of sound mind has at least once been a customer. Going to the shop where there are many new things on display, which item will attract you most? The most well packaged.

A vision also needs to be well packaged for it to be easily shared out.

The following are some of the features you need to incorporate in it for it to be appealing to those you desire to share with:

- It should be capable of being handled (short, clear, concise, understandable)
- It should be within reach (capable of being shared out)
- It should communicate a strong purpose
- It should be authentically compelling (being able to genuinely bring forth emotional attachment)
- It should subtly and covertly answer the question, "what is in it for me?"
- It should have utility (reach the right place, at the right time, in the right form)

On your psychedelic trip, draw from the well of creativity to bring forth that which quenches your audience's thirst for inspiration.

6. *Share out your dream*

It is not a great vision if it isn't sharable.

The worth of a vision rests in its ability to involve others. The following are some of the ways by which you can cause your vision to be shared out:

- Post it in mass media, especially social media
- Engage with recipients to create a positive relationship
- Form groups and communities of interests, each covering a specific area that needs to be implemented
- Rally people towards your vision – you can achieve this by using publicity, Public Relations, among others.

Leverage the power of emotional connectedness gained from the mystic shrooms to create a mastermind alliance towards your dream.

7. *Make it happen*

Actualize your vision. Enliven it by living it.

Begin to live as though you have already achieved your vision. It is not that every element of your vision will have been achieved. But, don't wait for everything to unravel. Start actualizing what can be actualized… and do update those you share your vision with.

Most importantly, know that actualization begins in the mind. Transform your mindset to align with your vision. Change your habits, attitude, and beliefs to align with your vision. Align your posture and behaviors with your vision.

Yes, let people feel that you are deeply in it. Only then can you begin to share with them the present of your vision.

Cast the new reality achieved on your visualized psychedelic trip onto your ground to guide your every step towards your goal. Let your steps be boldly assured in order to win the minds of the Doubting Thomas.

14

HOW TO TAP INTO THE PSYCHEDELIC POWER OF SHROOMS TO RESET AND REPROGRAM YOUR MINDSET

We've seen the power of psychedelic mushrooms in terms of reconnecting parts of your brains and transforming your mind. So far, we have not engaged in a deliberate exploration of the nature of the mind. However, it would be unjust to conclude this book without exploring the nature of the mind so that we gain an in-depth appreciation of the power of magic mushroom.

The mind is a complex subject to cover that requires an entire library of books on its own. However, we are going to explore the mind in very brief notes but without unduly sacrificing the need to understand the concepts. This way, we can be able to appreciate how the magic in the shrooms can facilitate the transformation of your mind to bring forth a new reality.

WHAT IS THE MIND?

This question elicits a lot of debate. It is one of those controversial areas where a clear-cut answer never comes forth. However, amidst the darkness, there is still a path. Some say that the mind is a part of the soul ("the soul's intelligence") while others say that the mind is a part of the heart ("the heart's intelligence"). Nonetheless, there is a common consensus that the mind is a part of the brain, and thus "brain's intelligence".

In this book, we pursue that common notion that the mind is a part of the brain. In this common notion, the mind is considered a functional part of the brain responsible for the memory of the past experiences, a set of instructions on how to detect the recurrence of that experience or similar experiences, and a set of instructions on what to do should it recur.

This set of instructions is what is commonly referred to as the mindset (how the mind is set to respond to various scenarios based on experience).

The best way to simplify our understanding of the mind's complexity is through analogies.

There are two analogies that best describes the mind's attributes – the Computer analogy, and the Library analogy.

The computer analogy – the best way to understand the programmable part of the mind

The best way to understand the nature of the mind is to compare it with the computer. In essence, the brain is a biochemical supercomputer. As such, the mind is a part of this computer. Our entire being is like a biochemical robot. So, just as a computer controls the rest of the robot body, does the brain controls the rest of our body.

We are now in the era of Artificial Intelligence and Machine Learning. One thing to learn from robots is that for a robot to work autonomously, there has to be sensors on different parts of its body – to sense the environment and respond appropriately based on the software instructions within the computer. We can equate these sensors to our nerves. All over our body are various nerves that sense the environment and feed the brain with data which it acts upon to instruct the body on what to do... based on the mindset. Thus, the mind is akin to the software part of a computer.

Just as a computer has both the hardware part and the software part, the brain has the "hardware" (the physical part) and software (the mind/mindset).

The physical part of the brain has a network of neurons (brain circuitry). This brain circuitry can be rewired through neuroplasticity. We've seen how psilocin works to rewire the brain circuitry through neuroplasticity. In this chapter, we will see how the mind/mindset can be reprogrammed through mindset reprogramming techniques.

The library analogy – the best way to understand our memory

Every library has a coding and tagging system to enable both librarians and readers to easily trace a book out of the thousands of books on the dozens of shelves. Without this coding and tagging system, it would be hard for the library to be organized and much harder for readers to get the books they need to read.

Every library has a register. This register has a record of all books. Within the register, each book has a title, author, publisher, volume, edition, etc. These are also represented in a unique book code. In addition to the unique book code, there is a location code that has information on the exact position where the book is located in the library. This location is indicated in terms of the shelf unit, shelf number, and the order number of the book within that particular shelf. In essence, this location code is the book's map. Thus, each book has a unique code, which is a combination of book code + location code.

Each book has a tag on it that displays its unique code. The reader can add more temporary codes to guide her while reading the book. These could include bookmarks, yellow tags, etc.

The purpose of the tag is to guide a reader to a particular memory (collection of information). A book is simply a collection of information. As such, it is physical memory.

Now, with this analogy, we can easily understand how our memory works. Our memory has registers, memory tags, memory labels (placed on the tags), mental maps (location maps), and mental images (mind books).

Also, our memory has a mindset that guides the action part of the brain on what mental image to fetch, where to fetch it from, how to fetch it, and what to do with it.

Our mind books are commonly known as mental images because they are more than the 'ordinary' books that we know.

For example, in a given instance of experience, a mental image will store such things as the sight of our experience, the smell of our experience, the taste of our experience, the actions and reactions of our experience, the environment of our experience, lessons learned, and a snippet of instructions of what to do should such an experience recur. These are more than what an 'ordinary' book can store.

We can compare this mental image to what we refer to in computers as an ISO image.

Yet, our mental image is much more than an ISO. It has data about the experience of our five senses concerning a given occurrence, how the brain reacted to this data, and future instructions of what to do when there is such recurrence.

The software analogy – the best way to understand our mindset

In this computer analogy, our mindset is software. This mindset interacts with various registers (memories) just as computer software interacts with various memory registers. The bulk of software comprises of stored procedures. Stored procedures are simply a stored set of instructions on what to do, step-by-step, should a given scenario recur. The stored procedures are automatically triggered by the occurrence of an event (as signaled). Only an external or counter intervention can stop this automatic mode from triggering or following the set pattern (mind map).

In this regard, we can consider the mind to be that part of the memory where the mindset exists. Oftentimes, mind and mindset are used interchangeably. However, this software analogy shows us that there is a difference between the two. The mind is a virtual container (or virtual memory) that holds the mindset. Sometimes the mindset is talked of as the 'programmable part of the mind'.

TYPES OF MIND

We can classify the mind either in 'storage form' or in the 'behavioral' form. In the 'storage' form, there are primarily three types of mind – Unconscious mind, subconscious mind, and the conscious mind.

In the 'behavioral' form, we do have a growth mindset and a fixed mindset. We have already seen what these two are in the previous chapters. We will still tackle them in greater depth later.

Why do we need to know these different types of minds?

Each of these minds plays a unique role. For example, the bulk of your permanent routine is etched in the unconscious mind. Semi-permanent routines such as those that you adopt for the sake of handling a short-term situation are registered in the subconscious mind. The conscious mind deals mainly with managing the execution of the routine as triggered within the unconscious or subconscious mind.

THE PROGRAMMABLE NATURE OF THE MIND

As we have seen from both the computer and library analogies, the mind(mindset) is programmable. Thus, you can reprogram or rewire your mind. This is the greatest nature of the mind.

Like any program and like any rewiring, whenever the performance is not optimal, you can do fault-finding to search for short-circuiting - defects, and malware that make it not function optimally.

It will be rather unfortunate for us to continue with our discussion assuming perfect minds. This would be rather ideal than real. In reality, mind, as part of our brain, is not immune to disease just as our other parts of the body. As such, it is important to be able to know how to tell when our minds ail and thus cease to be optimally functional.

While we may not be able to dwell deep into each mind rewiring technique, it is important to mention these techniques for your further research.

MINDSET REPROGRAMMING TECHNIQUES

The following are some of the mind reprogramming techniques that you need to explore more about:

- Neuroplasticity
- Mindfulness Meditation
- Creative Visualization
- Neuro-Linguistic Programming (NLP)

- Positive Thinking
- Positive Affirmations

These techniques can leverage the power of psilocybin to deliver faster and more effective outcomes. Psilocybin helps to loosen attachment to the faulty mental maps that we have created out of our experiences. It achieves this by dissolving the old patterns of thought and behavior and thus opening up a unique opportunity for the mind to be reprogrammed.

Ancient religious gurus, while acting as trip-sitters and teachers, employed mindfulness meditation, creative visualizations, and positive affirmations to rewire the mind of their students (trippers) to achieve a renewed state of mind.

With the knowledge that you have already acquired in the previous chapters about the power of psilocybin in terms of resetting, rewiring, and rebooting the brain, you can easily see how these techniques work in tandem with the magic in the shrooms to achieve a faster, more efficient and highly effective mind reprogramming.

RESETTING YOUR MINDSET USING NEUROPLASTICITY

Neuroplasticity is the act of rewiring the brain to snap it out of the brain lock. Dr. Schwartz, a renowned neuroscientist, formulated the famous Four Ways process as a technique of dealing with brain lock.

The brain lock

Brain lock is a neural condition in which the brain is locked in an 'on' state. It is like pressing a bell button that remains stuck inside – there will be constant ringing even though you no longer want it to ring. Brain lock effect is best witnessed in patients suffering from OCD. In this condition, the victim repeats mundane tasks such as frequently going to wash hands, frequently going to check the door just to confirm that it is locked, etc.

In the brain lock, a given thought is locked 'on' such that it keeps on appearing recursively. The best remedy to deal with brain lock is neuroplasticity.

Psilocin as brain unlocker

What psilocin does is to unlock the brain. In the introductory chapters, we saw that psilocin rewires the brain neurons by reactivating dormant neurons, repairing damaged neurons, and creating new connections, thus enabling parts of the brains that were hitherto not communicating well to do so in an optimized way.

The Four Ways Process (4Rs)

The four-way as a method of rewiring the mind has been advocated by Dr. Schwartz. These four ways are:

- Relabel – Relabeling is about retraining your mind to distinguish between a real thought and a non-real thought so that you are capable of assigning labels to each class of thoughts. This way, you can ignore non-real thoughts and focus your energies on dealing with real thought.
- Reattribute – after relabeling, you recognize that the non-

real thoughts are unnecessary noise distracting you from focusing your energies on the real thoughts. Thus, you can grant them an attribute 'unnecessary noise,' which allows you to easily filter them out of your thought processing.

- Refocus – once you have relabeled and reattributed your thoughts, you can concentrate and refocus your energies on what matters most – real thoughts. Whenever non-real thought comes up, you quickly refocus your attention away from it and towards the real thought.

- Revalue – in the revaluing process, you give value or essence to the real thought and deny value or essence to the non-real noisy thought. This revaluing involves assigning thought-processing energy to real thought while denying the same to non-real noisy thought.

These are the 4Rs, as advocated by Dr. Schwarz in his neuroplasticity approach. However, if you observe keenly at this 4-step process, you will realize that it is a more refined form that has picked some of the essential elements of mindfulness meditation and NLP. Indeed, NLP is just but a different attempt at neuroplasticity. Thus, these approaches – mindfulness meditation, NLP, Positive thinking, and 4Rs have a common bond and can greatly complement each other as techniques that can enable you to achieve a great result in resetting your mindset and, in effect, your subconscious mind.

The Four Ways Plus One

The Four Ways Plus One is simply the 4Rs we have discussed above plus one R (Re-create). To Re-create simply means re-creating or reforming your inner being anew. In this way, you can create a new being based on the outcome of the Four Ways process that involves the 4Rs.

The learned non-use

One of Schwarz's prominent research findings was that the brain reorganizes itself depending on its usage. Thus, whenever there a part of your body, including the brain itself, which is not being put into use, the brain learns not to use it. It is excluded from the active mental circuitry system. A kind of short circuitry happens to exclude it. Your mind too can get accustomed to learned nonuse, whereby some of its power rests in the subconscious mind because you have not been utilizing it. For example, the power of intuition is such great. The so-called prophets, foreseers, are people who have learned to dig deeper into this mind power. You too have this potential, but, because you have not accustomed yourself to exploit that deeper intuition, you have not exploited this potential, and thus the mind has cultivated this learned nonuse. Psilocin reconnects the isolated neurons that had hitherto been disconnected due to non-use.

It is so natural that your conscious mind will always bring forth thoughts depended on their ability to be used. Those thoughts that cannot be frequently utilized will rest in the subconscious mind, while those who have no utility at all will be driven deeper into the uncon-scious mind whereby extreme energy will have to be expended to resuscitate them from that 'dead' status to an awoken status.

Learned non-use is quite obvious in our daily lives. You will find people who are extremely poor, yet they are overwhelmed by rich natural resources. They starve, yet they have extremely fertile lands. They go thirsty, yet there are rivers and four rainfall seasons. There are learned non-use of the rich resources available within their means. They have simply not utilized their intuitive power of imagination that rests within their subconscious mind.

Focused attention – the greatest tool of neuroplasticity

The subconscious mind is a mind in darkness. Without it being illuminated through focused attention, it remains in darkness. Yet, the power of this focus must continually become intense for you to dig deeper into and beyond the subconscious mind – the right to the depth of unconscious mind so that which rests 'buried' in the unconscious mind can be transformed into the potential in the subconscious mind and further transformed into kinetic in the conscious mind.

Taking a micro-dose of the magic shrooms can help intensify this focused attention.

The power of this focused attention does exist in the physical realms. Lenses are known to concentrate light power. When this light power is directed onto paper, the paper lights up and burns. LASER (Light Amplification by Stimulated Emission of Radiation) is such a widely used physics technology that emanates for the power of focused attention. The light is focused through a chemical liquid medium on a straight path and is bounced back by deflection of the prism wall. Every time the light passes and bounces back through the liquid prism, it gets more intense (amplified).

Laser light has been known to be used to cut hard metals like diamonds, performs incisions during surgery, and cut materials such a paper, metal sheets, fabrics into required sizes. Such power of focused attention! Just take your subconscious mind as this liquid prism through which of knowledge from your external world is focused through and acquires more energy from the properties of your subconscious mind such that more and more knowledge of intense quality comes forth – what a genius process! The light is energy. Your thoughts are quantum bits of vibrating energy. Light amplification, whether through lenses or prism, occurs due to the process of excitation or bombardment of phantoms within the light, which causes higher rates of vibrations and greater magnitude. Your thoughts too are energies that can be excited and amplified in the same way to get higher magnitude, which is simply power – yes, power of thinking!

Your subconscious mind is these lenses. Your subconscious mind is this laser prism. It has those properties that can excite your thought energy to higher states of vibration, thus releasing more power. It only requires your focused attention. A story is frequently told of Buddhist monks who can focus their attention on the glass until it shatters; on a spoon until it bends. Miracles? Yes, miracles, if you don't understand the power of focused attention. Yet, this property called 'miracle' rests deep within your subconscious mind and only require stimuli – redirecting your quality thoughts through it again and again so that it gains higher power. Studying is based on this simple concept. The more you read and reread a given content, the better understanding, and mastery of its concepts manifest. Why? Because the good thought keeps on being bounced back through the amplification medium – your subconscious mind, each time gaining higher energy levels.

RESETTING YOUR MINDSET THROUGH MINDFULNESS MEDITATION

We have already discussed mindfulness and meditation in Chapter 13. While there is a lot to discuss in as far as mindfulness meditation is concerned as a mind rewiring tool, this is beyond the scope of this book. For now, what we have discussed about psychedelic meditation is sufficient for our psychedelic exploration.

RESETTING YOUR MINDSET THROUGH CREATIVE VISUALIZATION

Creative visualization is a cognitive process where one deliberately generates visual mental imagery for purposes of recreating or simulating visual perception to interrogate, enhance and transform those images with the intent of remapping associated mental tags or reprogramming associated interpretations to achieve and experience ensuing psychological, physiological, emotional or social benefits or effects.

Some of these beneficial effects include:

- Minimizing physical pain
- Healing wounds to the body
- Remedying psychological pain such as trauma, stress, anxiety, depression, sadness, and poor mood.
- Boosting self-confidence and self-esteem
- Improving coping mechanism in difficult social relations

Mental imagery – visual and non-visual

Through neuroplasticity (or simply reprogramming the brain), you are capable of creating different types of mental imagery distinct from visual imagery, thus recreating or simulating the intended experience of perception cutting across all sensory domains/modalities.

Some of these sensory modalities include:

- Olfactory imagery of smells
- Haptic imagery of touch (e.g., texture, pressure, temperature [hot, warm, cold, frozen, etc.])
- Auditory imagery of sounds
- Motor imagery of movements
- Gustatory imagery of tastes

Creative visualization is closely related to guided imagery in the sense that guided imagery is that part of creative visualization where an external party (a teacher) directs a student (the one carrying out creative visualization) to evoke and generate certain mental images that re-create or simulates sensory perception of either one or several specific sensory modalities.

In the entheogenic trip, the trip-sitter acts as the teacher while the tripper acts as the student. When shrooms are used for religious purposes, the priest becomes the teacher.

STAGES OF CREATIVE VISUALIZATION

Stage 1: Image generation

At this stage, mental imagery is evoked or generated from memory, imagination (fantasy), or both.

Stage 2: Image Maintenance

At this stage, deliberate effort is directed towards sustaining or maintaining generated imagery. Generated imagery is usually temporary unless deliberately sustained. Maintenance is important to ensure that the imagery process is transitioned to the next stage – inspection.

Stage 3: Image inspection

At this stage, the maintained image is inspected for clarity, explored for its various dimensions, and interpreted. This involves scanning the image in all its dimensions to derive its possible interpretations by the participant.

Stage 4: Image transformation

At this stage, the participant modifies, alters, or transforms the mental imagery through either remapping or reprogramming or both. Remapping involves recreating the image to a new image that suits a certain specific meaning. Reprogramming involves recreating the interpretation associated with particular mental imagery.

RESETTING YOUR MINDSET USING NLP TECHNIQUE

NLP can help you achieve a better life in terms of your purifying your inner being, enhancing your personal development, healing, and developing your relationships and thus enable you to achieve a wholeness of wellbeing.

What is NLP?

You have probably heard of the miraculous three-letter acronym NLP! In case this is the first time you hear about it, I am going to explain it all right here before you.

NLP stands for Neuro-Linguistic Programming. As the name suggests NLP has three core components;

1. Neurology
2. Language
3. Programming

Neurology is a derivative of the word 'neuro'. The word 'neuro' comes from the Greek word 'neuron' which refers to nerve while the suffix 'logy' is a derivative of the Greek word 'logia' which simply means 'study of'. Therefore, we can say that neurology is the study of nerves. However, scientifically, neurology is designated as a medical practice that chiefly concerns itself with the diagnosis and treatment of all illnesses that are directly or indirectly associated with the central nervous system.

Language refers to the human system of communication that uses either, some, or all of the several modes of expression such as speaking, writing, or gesturing to express inner thoughts or emotions to make sense of abstract and complex thought. Language is important in enabling us to communicate with one another, satisfy our needs and desires, and establish and maintain our relationships, culture, and traditions.

Programming refers to the action and or process of setting up predetermined behavioral patterns.

Programming is indeed the miracle glue that binds Neuro with Linguistic. When it blends with Neuro-Linguistic, it gets a much bigger dimension transcending all the contaminants of the mind. It simply liberates the mind from its imprisonment by creating a map that establishes a path to the mind's freedom.

Having these basic definitions of the core terms sets us up to dissect what NLP is all about. ***NLP is the art and science that chiefly concerns itself with the study and understanding of how people organize their thought, feelings, communications, and behavior to derive their outcomes***.

In simple language, we can say that NLP helps us to dissect the relationship between how we think (neuro), how we communicate our thoughts (linguistic), and the patterns of our behavior and emotions (programs).

The fundamental concept of NLP

The fundamental concept of NLP is that people derive unique mental maps of their environment as an outcome of how they filter and perceive information captured through their five senses. In this regard, the word 'neuro' has a unique meaning and which refers to the mental map which is derived from an individual's unique mental filtering system for processing data captured by the five senses. This mental map could constitute elements such as smells, tastes, sounds, internal images, and awareness that forms out an individual's neuro-logical filtering process. In NLP terminology, this mental map is commonly known as 'First Access'.

Just as neuro, linguistic has a unique meaning to NLP and simply refers to assigning personal meaning to information gathered from the environment. This linguistic process populates the Linguistic Map by assigning language to smells, tastes, sounds, feelings, and internal images, thus resulting in a heightened degree of conscious awareness. This Linguistic Map is the second map of NLP.

NLP is about creating mental maps. Indeed, any journey you embark on is about making footsteps along the carpet that your mind map unfolds right before your feet. You can never make a voluntary foot-step without a mental map. Yes, you could be doing so subconsciously not to realize it, but so true it is.

THE CORE FUNDAMENTALS OF NLP;

NLP revolves around these three fundamentals:

Subjectivity – each one of us sees the world in a different light.

Maps – our worlds are made of boundaries and territories that our life experiences draw out for us. A map is only a representation of a place and not the place itself.

Language – we have the power to redraw and expand those boundaries using mind manipulation systems, language being the most effective manipulator.

The core principles of NLP that you should keep in mind are:

- Other people's models of the world are not necessarily wrong
- The meaning of communication is the response it produces
- Everyone does the best they can with the resources available to them
- You are in control of your mind and hence your result
- People are not their behaviors and neither are they their relationships

RESETTING YOUR MINDSET THROUGH POSITIVE THINKING

Positive thinking is a mental attitude that focuses on the better nature of being and visualizes the benefits that come from this nature.

The greatest secret of life is that no one was born to experience misery. No one was purposely born to live an unhappy life. We were all born to experience joy and happiness. However, due to some causes within or beyond our control, joy, happiness, and success have proven elusive due to the negativities that have shrouded our minds. Yet, in our mind rests the key to igniting optimism, success, and happiness. We only need to ignite this by starting positively.

To start positively is to look at your compass and find direction to where you ought to be. Only then can you make a move that is not an aimless wander. This too begins in the mind. You have to initiate a thought. This thought has to come from an understanding of its need to be. So, to start positively in positive thinking is to engage your mind to first understand what it is before giving it the right direction – a positive direction.

In this world full of competition, with success having been commoditized, sometimes you can feel overwhelmed if you can't fit the bill that is the price tag of this commoditized success. Success has become a product in the market whose value is determined by how much it fetches in monetary terms. This leaves many, whose success is not 'marketable' to feel frustrated and think negatively of themselves and, at times, about everything around them.

Positive thinking helps to bring out the original sense of success. A success that is not measurable by momentary gains. A success that is so unique that can't be put on a comparative and competitive scale of measure. It is in this original sense of success that we find our true nature – where we come to understand that we are uniquely and wonderfully created, and we have full potential inherent within us to achieve our unique purposes in life.

Positive thinking enables you to bring out the best in you, which you can share with the rest of humanity. Without optimism, the will to do this becomes overwhelming. Positive thinking invigorates your optimism, which boosts your will to explore and exploit your potential.

Positive thinking has immense benefits.

Appreciate the immense benefits of positive thinking

Studies continue to come up with the benefits of positive thinking. The following are some of the proven benefits of positive thinking;

- **Increased lifespan** – studies have shown that those people who engage in positive thinking have higher chances of living longer than those who engage in negative thinking.
- **Better coping ability to hardships, disasters, and distress** – Several studies have been carried out to establish how those who practice positive thinking fair on in difficult situations such as prisons, bereavement, natural disasters, wars, etc. compared to those who do not. These studies have found out that those people with positive thinking have a better coping mechanism for such situations, unlike those who don't practice positive thinking.
- **Lower rates of mental disorders** – people who practice positive thinking are less susceptible to stress, anxiety, depression, and other forms of mental disorders, unlike those who don't practice positive thinking.
- **Higher levels of immunity** – those who practice positive thinking have a higher level of immunity. This makes them less susceptible to conditions such as common cold and allergies.

- **Reduced risks of death due to cardiovascular disease** – several research findings have established that people who practice positive thinking have a lower risk of cardiovascular disease as opposed to those who don't.
- **Better wholesome wellbeing** – those who practice positive thinking are wholesomely better off than those who don't. Thus, they experience higher levels of satisfaction, joy, and happiness plus overall longevity.

Sometimes it is not easy to just assume that you can naturally stay positive. It needs the effort to achieve these. The following are some of the ways on how you can stay manage to stay positive:

- **Identify key areas that you need to make changes** – you have to critically observe your attitude, beliefs, and habits. Those that implant negative thoughts must be weeded out.
- **Check your wellbeing** – while your mind affects the rest of your body, your mind too can receive pressure from your body. Checking your overall wellbeing is important in achieving overall wellbeing. Check your diet, check your fitness and everyday activity to determine whether they help bring out the best of you or not. You have to avoid those things that don't help to bring out the best of you.
- **Be open to humor and laugher** – they say humor and laughter are the best medicine of the soul. A happy soul will naturally trigger a positive mind. Entertain yourself. Laugh

often and much. Expose yourself to situations that make that come out naturally.

- **Live a healthy lifestyle** – a healthy lifestyle is a one that doesn't cause any part of your wellbeing to suffer or become diseased.
- **Surround yourself with positive people** – happiness radiates positive effects on others. If you surround yourself with positive people, you receive positive energies that boost your optimism and make you see things from a positive perspective.
- **Practice positive affirmation** – positive affirmation is one such great technique in which you seek to influence your mind through the power of feedback via your words. It reinforces the positive effect in your mind, thus helping to suppress and avoid negative thoughts from overwhelming you.

RESETTING YOUR MINDSET THROUGH POSITIVE AFFIRMATIONS

Positive affirmations are positively-framed personal statements about who you are, as ought to be, in the moment of now.

Thus, positive affirmations take the present tense since they are not framed about what you will be in the future but about who you are now as ought to be.

Positive affirmation simply follows the maxim 'what you think is what you become'. Thus, you seek to affirm the best of you, as ought to be, through the power of your words. This pushes your mind to focus on your words and deal with them rather than receding to the darkness of negativity.

Know why you need positive affirmations

Many people hardly comprehend how the mind works. The mind depends so much on the stored program that is deeply embedded in your memory. Your mind depends so much on this program (mindset) to interpret the present. This mindset (mental map) consists mostly of your past – your experiences, traditions, teachings, and even some subtle occurrences that happened in the past that you were not consciously aware of. Unfortunately, sometimes this program may contain negative codes (otherwise known as 'bugs' in a programming language) that may hinder your mind's productivity, thus constraining your potential.

To carry out positive affirmation is to erase these negative codes or kill the bugs so that you remain with a pristine program (mindset) that optimizes your potential.

From this simple analogy, it is easy to deduce some of the reasons as to why you need positive affirmations. The following reasons easily come out:

1. To get rid of the defective mindset that limits your potential
2. To rewrite (re-code) your mindset so that you can fill the void left by the negative thoughts (bugs) with positive codes.
3. To keep testing your mindset, refining and reinforcing your positive thinking power

4. To provide no room (fissures) for negative thoughts (bugs) to creep in

5. To keep on activating your mindset (software) so that it can be dependable in running your tasks (body activities)

6. To achieve your highest aspirations – dreams and visions

7. To help others achieve their potential through compassion – sharing the rewards of positive thinking

For more information on the positive affirmation (part of positive thinking) read specialized books on the same.

CONCLUSION

Thank you for acquiring this book and reading it through to this point.

I hope the information provided in this book has enabled you to enjoy your psychedelic trip experiences. I also hope that through these great trip experiences, you have been inspired enough to start your magic garden to guarantee your supply of quality psychedelic shrooms.

Due to legal restrictions regarding the growing and consumption of psilocybin mushrooms, there isn't enough publicity about this nature's wonder-world hidden under the tiny umbrella of grounded shrooms. Many will be getting to know these magic mushrooms for the first time through this book. If you are that lucky, kudos! Nonetheless, some have already had the benefit of knowledge about these mushrooms well before acquiring this book. To all the readers, there is great value for you.

Why psilocybin mushrooms? The book has answered this question adequately. I hope you are satisfied with the brief information that could be pumped into this book. The answer to this fundamental question has covered the nature of psilocybin mushrooms, their therapeutic benefits, and why they are ideal for you.

If you have never been inspired to keep a garden in your home, well, this is the time. Magic mushroom is your source of this inspiration. In this book, I have informed you why you need to grow your psilocybin mushrooms, potential places to grow them in your home, and how to grow them so that you gain the highest potency possible.

Every gardener knows that harvesting time is the reward time. To optimize your reward – not just to reap the dividends of your sheer effort of investing in your garden - but also to cap your dividends with a bonus, I have shown you how to harvest your mushrooms. I have gone further to demonstrate to you how to cure and store your psilocybin mushrooms so that their potency is not lost to the vagaries of nature.

Harvesting is one part, but the joy of it all is when the rewards of your effort unveil to you a miraculous trip to paradise. All your effort amounts to naught if you cannot arrive at your destiny – psychedelic heaven. Even with great faith and best effort, without proper direction, you may end up going to the wrong destiny. You do not deserve a psychedelic hell due to a bad trip. This is why I have taken time to show you different ways to consume your psychedelic mushrooms so that you do not miss out on the entheogenic paradise. In this endeavor, I have unveiled to you the different methods of consuming the magic shrooms, how to take the right dose of your magic, and how to refuel your body so that you are sufficiently energized to complete your trip.

Last but not least, the psychedelic lifestyle is not about just one or a few trips. It is not about momentarily living in a psychedelic bubble and clinging to its walls till it bursts. Psychedelic lifestyle is about transforming your entire life so that you can actualize your psychedelic ideas and live your psychedelic dreams. It is big misery if you happen to go to heaven, and after its angelic enjoyment, you come back to hell. To avoid this misery, you need to engender a psychedelic lifestyle. A psychedelic lifestyle is about bringing that heavenly experience into this worldly reality so that you can transform it. And psychedelic lifestyle is about transforming your worldly being to be that of an almost omnipotent and omniscient being that you became while in the psychedelic paradise.

All in all, my ultimate intention is for you to live a psychedelic lifestyle.

Good Luck!